MUSEUM OF MODERN ART
TENTH LOAN EXHIBITION

LAUTREC   REDON

FEBRUARY 1   1931   MARCH 2

730 FIFTH AVENUE · NEW YORK

REPRINT EDITION, 1969   PUBLISHED FOR THE MUSEUM OF MODERN ART BY ARNO PRESS

REPRINT EDITION, 1969   ARNO PRESS
LIBRARY OF CONGRESS CATALOG CARD NO. 71-86435

THE EXHIBITION HAS BEEN SELECTED FROM THE FOLLOWING COLLECTIONS:

MR. JAMES W. BARNEY, NEW YORK
MR. ALEXANDER M. BING, NEW YORK
MRS. CORNELIUS N. BLISS, JR., NEW YORK
MISS L. P. BLISS, NEW YORK
F. H. BRESLER COMPANY, MILWAUKEE
MR. WALTER S. BREWSTER, CHICAGO
MR. GERALD BROOKS, NEW YORK
MR. JOHN NICHOLAS BROWN, PROVIDENCE, RHODE ISLAND
MRS. JOHN ALDEN CARPENTER, CHICAGO
MR. THOMAS COCHRAN, NEW YORK
MR. AND MRS. RALPH M. COE, CLEVELAND
MR. AND MRS. CHESTER DALE, NEW YORK
MESSRS. DURAND-RUEL, NEW YORK AND PARIS
MR. FRANK H. GINN, CLEVELAND
MR. A. CONGER GOODYEAR, NEW YORK
MR. CARTER H. HARRISON, CHICAGO
MR. WILLIAM PRESTON HARRISON, LOS ANGELES
MR. PHILIP HOFER, NEW YORK
MR. JOHN A. HOLABIRD, CHICAGO
MESSRS. M. KNOEDLER AND COMPANY, NEW YORK, LONDON AND PARIS
MR. PAUL LAMB, CLEVELAND
MR. ADOLPH LEWISOHN, NEW YORK
MR. AND MRS. SAMUEL A. LEWISOHN, NEW YORK
MRS. FRANK R. LILLIE, CHICAGO
MR. ALBERT E. McVITTY, BRYN MAWR, PENNSYLVANIA
MRS. CHARLES J. MARTIN, MINNEAPOLIS
MRS. JAMES B. MURPHY, NEW YORK
MR. J. B. NEUMANN, NEW YORK
MRS. DIODATA O'TOOLE, NEW YORK
MESSRS. ALEXANDER REID & LEFÈVRE, LONDON
MRS. JOHN D. ROCKEFELLER, JR., NEW YORK
MR. MARTIN A. RYERSON, CHICAGO
DR. B. D. SAKLATWALLA, CRAFTON, PENNSYLVANIA
MR. M. B. SANDERS, JR., NEW YORK
MR. HARDINGE SCHOLLE, NEW YORK
MESSRS. JACQUES SELIGMANN AND COMPANY, NEW YORK AND PARIS
MR. JOHN L. SENIOR, CHICAGO
MR. JOHN T. SPAULDING, BOSTON

DR. JOSEF STRANSKY, NEW YORK
MR. AND MRS. CORNELIUS J. SULLIVAN, NEW YORK
THE THANNHAUSER GALLERIES, BERLIN AND LUCERNE
DR. W. R. VALENTINER, DETROIT
MESSRS. WILDENSTEIN AND COMPANY, NEW YORK AND PARIS
THE ALBRIGHT ART GALLERY, BUFFALO
THE ART INSTITUTE OF CHICAGO
THE ART MUSEUM OF YALE UNIVERSITY, NEW HAVEN, CONNECTICUT
THE BOSTON MUSEUM OF FINE ARTS
THE BROOKLYN MUSEUM
THE DETROIT INSTITUTE OF ARTS
THE LOUVRE MUSEUM, PARIS
THE MINNEAPOLIS INSTITUTE OF ARTS
THE WORCESTER ART MUSEUM

In addition to those who have lent works of art, the Trustees and the Staff wish to thank the following for their generous co-operation in assembling the exhibition.

The Director, Mr. Robert B. Harshe and Mr. Daniel Catton Rich of the Art Institute of Chicago for their very special help in arranging the exhibition of the works of Henri de Toulouse-Lautrec.

M. Henri Verne of the Louvre Museum, Paris; Mr. Henry Sayles Francis; Mr. C. M. de Hauke; Mr. E. C. Holston; Miss Isabel Jarvis of The Arts Club of Chicago; Miss A. M. Kraushaar; Mr. William M. Milliken; Mr. Russel A. Plimpton; Mr. James St. L. O'Toole.

TRUSTEES

INTRODUCTION

"A flat face, a nose that has nothing Greek in it, eyes with a wild light in them, eyelids rather satanical, a heap of reddish hair, flat breasts: that's the woman." So wrote Goncourt of Yvette Guilbert. Beauty or rather the lack of it remained the paradox of the French Music Hall at the end of the century. There was much more of tragedy, even caricature of tragedy, in its songs and quadrilles. It was direct; it was cruel. Its artificial quality, if any, lay alone in the seriousness behind each re-creation. Nor was it strange that it thought cruelly of life more often than it sung of it gayly—they who sang and danced, the realness of life for them helped them build illusion of amazing certainty. It was not always comforting. It was rarely pretty. It was often merciless. Of true comedy there was very little.

"Yvette begins to sing and immediately the gay world that you see across the smoke of your cigarette seems to unmask itself, becomes too suddenly serious, tragic, a piece of real existence."[1] The gay world become tragic—that was the world of cabarets and cafés. That was the world Toulouse-Lautrec watched. It was the world he knew and painted.

Henri de Toulouse-Lautrec-Monfa was born at Albi, the 24th of November 1864. His father, the Count Toulouse-Lautrec, a direct descendent of the famous Counts of Toulouse, was a huntsman of no little enthusiasm, and an almost fanatical believer in the freedom of an outdoor life. Henri, a courageous youngster, though rather frail, might well have followed in his father's footsteps had he not at the age of fourteen met with a series of accidents that left him permanently crippled. As is not infrequent in life the inability to do often increases the interest in observation and Henri found himself in the position of being forced to watch much of a life for which he had considerable enthusiasm but in which little was left that he could enact. His was to remain apart from all this, the hunting, the horses, the hounds and with this early isolation he cultivated a surety of perception and an independence of mind which was later to be most valuable. He did not, however, even to the end, escape the inevitable limitations of this isolation for he remained even later in Montmartre always an outsider. He was never a part of it all. He would have liked it, but he was not of its people. Undoubtedly in that lay some portion of his power—he saw more

---

[1] Arthur Symons.

piercingly, he analyzed more carefully than could he had he been *within* the scene he watched night after night.

So Henri sketched the hounds but never followed them and in 1882 entered Bonnat's atelier in Paris. There followed a period of complete discouragement, for the independent Lautrec found himself continually at odds with the routine of the studio. It was only a little later at Cormon's that he met another disconsolate artist, Vincent van Gogh, but he was even then ready to cease his studies. Lautrec realized that he could not follow the Academy, he was not of its stamp and he would not conform. He solved the problem quickly and directly—he threw it all over, broke with his family and went to live in Montmartre.

He worked furiously, yet his life was, with all, simple and without sensational episodes. Night after night saw him at the Moulin-Rouge sketching—always making those countless drawings that were to be worked later into his paintings. The tempo gradually increased. There were hasty journeys to Spain. There was more of drink and less of care. Finally the mind broke and at thirty-five he entered a maison de santé. He recovered slightly to his friends' surprise and went to rest in the sun in the south of France. Here for a very brief period he painted a bit. But he was far from well.

He died at Malromé, September 9, 1901, in years still a young man.

"Nous découvrons maintenant que Lautrec ne nous paraissant surnaturel que parce qu'il était naturel à l'extrême." Thus Tristan Bernard sums up the work of the artist. His ability to see naturally stands him apart from those of his contemporaries who saw but who often dehumanized their impressions. The type, only as it was manifest in the individual, interested him and the individual he exposed to a ruthless, detailed observation which cut far below the surface. Through his friend the photographer Paul Sescau he studied the use of the camera as a means of portrayal. Nor was this strange. The camera saw directly, clearly. It could "freeze" action. It grasped reality. And that same snap-shot (Nos. 5, 7) quality of action so pertinent to the lens' eye which had influenced Degas influenced him.

But the objectivity of the camera was not enough. Whereas it only *recorded* Lautrec *sensed* and recorded. Whereas expression and movement were to the camera objective, to the artist they were, naturally, built upon something deeper. He had the uncanny ability, especially since one must recall that he was not born of this crowd on Montmartre, of knowing these people, of revealing the changing emotion within which motivates the expression without. He did not seek a simple common denominator of character for he knew the complication of the simplest emotion. He knew how close grotesqueness can be to beauty and how cruel thereby; he knew so well the tragic, tense, the almost artificial activity that comes of frustration and he saw always round about him the deadly seriousness of being gay. It is hardly remarkable (Nos. 3, 9, 11, 21, 23, 24, etc.) that his portraits are amazingly real. They devastate at times (No. 28) because Lautrec felt no desire to edit his keen analysis. He liked, instead, inequality in that rather bitter way that those who suffer it find to enjoy. He might paint till doom but he could never join the dancing and it was dancing he most wanted.

In 1892 Lautrec turned to lithography. It is not surprising in view of his draughtsmanship that, once he had mastered the technique, he became one of the greatest artists in that medium. It is possibly because of its intrinsic calligraphic quality (No. 12) that one does not sense a break in Lautrec's style between his oils and his drawings and lithographs. In manner they blend neatly. The latter he turned out in great numbers in subjects ranging all the way from courtroom scenes (Nos. 59, 60, 61) to decorations for theater programs (No. 50) and café menus. But though apparently quickly turned off much care went into their composition and design. Lautrec had discovered a kindred spirit in the great Eastern delineator of life, Hokusai, and from him he had learned a somewhat increased simplification of pattern and line. This simplification he found useful and to his liking in both his oils (No. 21) and lithographs.

Yet whatever his medium his subject matter remained the same—the music halls, cafés, cabarets. He became as much a part of that life as its singers and its dancers. But whereas the song had an ending and the dancing stopped Lautrec preserved some moment of it—sad, gay, tragic and so careful was his observation that it may be hard to say truthfully whether in memory those who heard and saw ultimately remembered as they had seen or as Lautrec had forced them to see. Nor is it simple (nor necessary, fortunately) to decide just where the artist's amazing imagination created in his subjects something which the painter subjectively and always, perhaps, a bit harshly, felt *should be there*. He summed their mannerisms and emotions far better than they could have done.

The life of that period has passed. There no longer exists in Paris its like. But Toulouse-Lautrec has left a record of it more real, more brilliant, even a bit more sad, than a song of Guilbert.

"I have tried to make them real," Lautrec once said of some of his drawings.

"I have tried unreality," Odilon Redon might well have replied for if the real existed for Lautrec the unreal, the world of weird dreams, was Redon's fascination. Yet they suffered some things in common—the restlessness of dissatisfaction in their early work and a feeling of rebellion against the academic standards of the day, and each had a vivid imagination though its direction had little in common.

Odilon Redon was born at Bordeaux, April 20, 1840. His early life as a student seems to have been that of a rather frantic search after that medium of creative expression of which he instinctively felt he might become master. He failed at the Beaux-Arts. He tried in succession architecture and sculpture. He swayed under the influence of Corot and Chintreuil, painting curious imitations of the Barbizon masters. He studied botany. He made countless drawings of insects, of butterflies. "Be always yourself," his drawing teacher had told him, yet in this formative period Redon lacked the courage or insight to throw all over and stand alone. He was miserable and he knew no remedy.

It was not until 1863 when he became interested in etching through his friend, Rudolphe Bresdin, that artist who has remained so strangely unknown and unappreciated, that we first note the courage to play with a composition in a fantastic way. The medium of etching is fairly flexible. The design etched on the copper plate may be burnished out and re-bitten, and other designs superimposed. It is in these changes of states of the print—this reworking of the plate—that we can watch reality disappear and fantasy grow in its place.

But while this medium offered some flexibility it was not as graphic a means of representation as lithography.[1] Nor did it allow such depths of black or such gradations of tone. So Redon turned to lithography and in 1879 under the technical guidance of Fantin-Latour he mastered its technique and published his first series of prints, *Dans le Rêve*. It was his renunciation of the bothersome world of actuality. From then on he busied himself with illustration. He sought the writings of Flaubert, Poe, Baudelaire. He became fascinated with the word and its power to build illusion, and out of this there grew the formation of a symbolic language—the dream face, the strange profile, horses with wings, mists, the arbitrary use of light and shade, strange insects, beautiful butterflies, and around all, endless space. In this period color disappears, its place taken by luminous blacks and greys, and his composition tends to become asymmetrical.

---

[1] Because of lack of space the lithographs of Odilon Redon are not shown in this exhibition.

It was not until the last seventeen years of his life that Redon began to work in oil, watercolor and pastel.[1] His long apprenticeship as a draughtsman had given him a remarkable security in design. For the paradox of unreality is the care with which the suggestion of it must be given. Now color comes into play, yet the palette is arbitrary—brilliant violets, oranges, blues. Flowers assume a strangeness although in all this later work form is there definitely. For the surety for form which Redon learned in his study of architecture contributes to the greatness of his work in giving him that remarkable ability to express real weight and volume in the curious balancing of unreal things.

Toulouse-Lautrec and Odilon Redon stand poles apart, yet our assertion of their fundamental differences of outlook is perhaps rendered less certain of definition when viewed in the light of Lautrec's interesting remark:

"When my hand starts going I have to let it go where it will."

J. A.

[1] Many of the works in this exhibition date from this period.

CATALOG

HENRI de TOULOUSE-LAUTREC

Henri de Toulouse-Lautrec-Monfa. Born in Albi 1864. Direct descendant of the Counts of Toulouse. His father, Count de Toulouse-Lautrec, worked at modeling as an amateur and knew the animal painters John Lewis Brown and René Princeteau. 1789, A series of accidents, leaving Henri a cripple. 1882, Paris, entered Bonnat's atelier. 1883, Met van Gogh. 1885, Turned against the Ecole des Beaux-Arts and took a studio in Montmartre with Grenier. Interest in cabarets, cafés, circuses. 1891, First colored poster. 1892, Interest in the East. 1895–1897, Paris and two Spanish journeys. Breakdown in health. 1899, Confinement in a maison de santé. Died 1901 at Malromé.†

NOTE: An asterisk before a catalog number indicates that the painting is illustrated by a plate which bears the same number.

1 PORTRAIT-SKETCH OF MADAME GRENIER (1885)‡
Oil on cardboard, 17½ x 12½ inches
Collection Carter H. Harrison, Chicago

*2 THE LOUIS XIII CHAIR AT BRUANT'S CABARET (1886)
Oil on cardboard mounted on canvas, 20½ x 31 inches
Collection Messrs. Durand-Ruel, New York and Paris

3 PORTRAIT OF ALINE GIBERT (1887)
Oil on canvas, 24 x 19¾ inches
Collection Mr. and Mrs. Ralph M. Coe, Cleveland

4 A MASKED BALL AT THE ELYSEE-MONTMARTRE (1887)
Oil on cardboard, 23⅜ x 18⅛ inches
Collection Messrs. M. Knoedler and Company, New York, London and Paris

*5 RIDERS ON THEIR WAY TO THE BOIS DE BOULOGNE (1888)
Black and white on cardboard, 33¼ x 19¾ inches
Collection Adolph Lewisohn, New York

† In the compilation of the Lautrec Catalog acknowledgment is made to the data kindly furnished by the Art Institute of Chicago.

‡ Titles and dates are according to Maurice Joyant, *Henri de Toulouse-Lautrec*, I, II, Paris, 1926 and 1927.

*6 LITTLE DOG (1888)

Oil on wood, 6¼ x 9⅛ inches
Collection William Preston Harrison, Los Angeles

*7 AT THE CIRCUS FERNANDO. THE RING MASTER (1888)

Oil on canvas, 38¾ x 63½ inches
Collection The Art Institute of Chicago (Joseph Winterbotham Collection)

*8 HEAD OF A WOMAN

Oil on cardboard, 13½ x 27 inches
Collection Paul Lamb, Cleveland

*9 WOMAN IN A STUDIO

Oil on canvas, 22 x 18 inches
Collection John T. Spaulding, Boston

*10 RUSSIAN WOMAN (1889)

Oil on cardboard, 28 x 23 inches
Collection The Albright Art Gallery, Buffalo

11 PORTRAIT OF BERTHE LA SOURDE (1890)

Oil on cardboard, 24 x 44 inches
Private collection, New York

*12 WOMAN SMOKING A CIGARETTE (1890)

Oil on cardboard, 18½ x 11¾ inches
Collection The Brooklyn Museum

*13 PORTRAIT OF PAUL SESCAU (1891)

Oil on paper, 39½ x 20¾ inches
Collection The Brooklyn Museum

14 WOMAN IN A GARDEN (1891)

Oil on cardboard, 23¾ x 21¾ inches
Collection Mr. and Mrs. Cornelius J. Sullivan, New York

*15 THE TOILETTE (1891)

Oil on cardboard, 28¾ x 25½ inches
Collection Mr. and Mrs. Cornelius J. Sullivan, New York

*16 LADY WITH A DOG

Oil on cardboard, 29 x 22½ inches
Collection Gerald Brooks, New York

*17 READING

Oil on cardboard, 27 x 23½ inches
Collection Adolph Lewisohn, New York

18 WOMAN'S HEAD

Oil on cardboard, 14 x 9½ inches
Collection Mr. and Mrs. Cornelius J. Sullivan, New York

*19 AT THE MOULIN-ROUGE (1892)

Oil on canvas, 55¼ x 47¼ inches
Collection The Art Institute of Chicago (The Birch-Bartlett Collection)

*20 THE QUADRILLE AT THE MOULIN-ROUGE (1892)

Pastel on cardboard, 31½ x 23¾ inches
The Chester Dale Collection, New York

*21 THE DIVAN (1893)

Oil on cardboard, 21⅛ x 27¼ inches
Collection Wildenstein and Company, New York and Paris

*22 JANE AVRIL DANCING (1893)

Oil on cardboard, 39¾ x 29 inches
Collection Wildenstein and Company, New York and Paris

*23 MISS MAY BELFORT (1895)

Oil on cardboard, 24½ x 19 inches
Private Collection, New York

*24 PORTRAIT OF MAY MILTON (1895)

Oil on cardboard, 25½ x 18¾ inches
Collection Walter S. Brewster, Chicago

*25 LA CLOWNESS CHA-U-KAO (1895)

Oil on cardboard, 32 x 23½ inches
Collection Frank H. Ginn, Cleveland

*26 THE MOORISH DANCE OR "LES ALMEES" (1895)

Oil on canvas, 118⅛ x 118⅛ inches
Collection The Louvre Museum, Paris

*27 THE DANCE AT THE MOULIN-ROUGE (1895)

Oil on canvas, 118⅛ x 118⅛ inches
Collection The Louvre Museum, Paris

*28 PORTRAIT OF OSCAR WILDE (1895)

Watercolor on paper, 24 x 19½ inches
Collection Messrs. Jacques Seligmann and Company, New York and Paris

*29 LADY AT THE PIANO (1896)

Oil on cardboard, 29½ x 23½ inches
Private Collection Josef Stransky, New York

30 PORTRAIT OF MAXIME DETHOMAS AT THE BAL DE L'OPERA (1896)

Oil on cardboard, 26½ x 20¾ inches
Collection Alexander Reid & Lefèvre, London

31 MADAME MISSIA NATANSON (1897)

Oil on cardboard panels mounted on wood, 32 x 38 inches
Collection Thannhauser Galleries, Berlin and Lucerne

32 PORTRAIT OF MADAME MISSIA NATANSON (1897)

Oil on cardboard, 21 x 16⅛ inches
Collection C. W. Kraushaar, New York

33 THE ENGLISH GIRL AT THE "STAR" AT LE HAVRE (1899)
Oil on cardboard, 18¼ x 13½ inches
Collection Mr. and Mrs. Cornelius J. Sullivan, New York

*34 MESSALINA (BORDEAUX, 1900)
Oil on canvas, 39 x 28½ inches
Collection Adolph Lewisohn, New York

DRAWINGS

35 THE MODEL NIZZAVONA (1883)
Charcoal on paper, 18½ x 24½ inches
Collection Carter H. Harrison, Chicago

*36 AU CAFÉ
Brush, ink and blue chalk on yellow paper, 26½ x 23¾ inches
Collection John Nicholas Brown, Providence, Rhode Island

37 THE BAR ON THE RUE DE ROME (1886)
Charcoal on paper, 12 x 15¾ inches
Collection Carter H. Harrison, Chicago

38 A DANCE AT THE MOULIN DE LA GALETTE (1889)
Chalk and china ink on brown paper, 34 x 38 inches
Collection James W. Barney, New York

39 LE PÈRE COTELL (1893)
Pencil, blue and red crayon and ink on cardboard, 20 x 13½ inches
Collection Carter H. Harrison, Chicago

40 THREE WOMEN (1894)
China ink on paper, 8½ x 13½ inches
Collection John L. Senior, Chicago

*41 SKATING: PROFESSIONAL BEAUTY (1896)
Drawing colored with gouache and crayon on paper, 25¾ x 20¾ inches
Collection Jacques Seligmann and Company, New York and Paris

*42 AT ARMENONVILLE (1896)

   Chinese ink with touches of blue crayon on tan paper, 25 ½ x 19¾ inches
   Collection The Minneapolis Institute of Arts (John de Laittre Memorial Collection)

DRY POINTS

   The following seven dry points of Lautrec's friends are from the Collection of Walter S. Brewster, Chicago.

43 THE EXPLORER, L. J., VICOMTE DE BRETTES? (1898), D. 2†

44 CHARLES MAURIN (1898), D. 3

   Charles Maurin was a French engraver.

45 FRANCIS JOURDAIN (1898), D. 4

   A French painter and engraver

46 W. H. B. SANDS (EDINBURGH EDITOR), (1898), D. 5 (Trial proof?)

47 HENRY SOMM (1898), D. 6. (Not described in Delteil)

   Henry Somm (Franoçis-Clement Sommier) was an illustrator and etcher

48 THE WRESTLER VILLE? (1898), D. 7

49 PORTRAIT OF M. X. . . . . (1898), D. 8

LITHOGRAPHS

50 THE COIFFEUR (1893), D. 14, I

   A program for the Theatre-Libre
   Private Collection, New York

51 SARAH BERNHARDT IN "PHEDRE" (1893), D. 47

   Collection C. W. Kraushaar, New York

52 AT THE AMBASSADEURS (1894), D. 68

   Private Collection, New York

† The classification is from Loys Delteil, *Le Peintre-Graveur Illustré*, Vols. X and XI, Paris, 1920. The roman numeral, where occuring, refers to the state.

18

53 "EROS VANNÉ" (1894), D. 74, II
Cover for a song by Maurice Donnay
Private Collection, New York

54 ANNA HELD IN "TOUTES CES DAMES AU THÉÂTRE" (1885), D. 100
Collection F. H. Bresler Company, Milwaukee

55 MISS MAY BELFORT, BOWING (1895), D. 117
Private Collection, New York

56 CLÉO DE MÉRODE (1895), D. 152
From a portfolio of thirteen lithographs of actors and actresses
Collection C. W. Kraushaar, New York

57 ÉMILIENNE D'ALENÇON, D. 161
From the portfolio of actors and actresses
Collection C. W. Kraushaar, New York

58 CASSIVE, D. 162
From the portfolio of actors and actresses
Private Collection, New York

Three lithographs from the Elles Album, 1896

59 PROCÈS ARTON (First Plate), (DÉPOSITION DUPAS), (1896), D. 191

60 PROCÈS ARTON (Second Plate), (DÉPOSITION RIBOT), (1896), D. 192

61 PROCÈS ARTON (Third Plate), (DÉPOSITION SOUDAIS), (1896), D. 193
The three lithographs from the Collection of J. B. Neumann, New York

62 THE OLD HORSE (1898), D. 224
Private Collection, New York

63 MARCELLE LENDER EN BUSTE, DE TROIS QUARTS (1898), D. 261
Collection The Museum of Fine Arts, Boston

64 JANE AVRIL AT THE JARDIN DE PARIS (1893), D. 345, I
   Private Collection, New York

65 NAPOLEON (1895), D. 357, I
   Executed for a composition to advertise *History of Napoleon I* by Father Sloane
   Collection C. W. Kraushaar, New York

66 JANE AVRIL (1899), D. 367, II
   Private Collection, New York

SOME OF LAUTREC'S CHARACTERS*

DANCERS

JANE AVRIL ("La Mélinite") of the *quadrille quartette*. Nicknamed for a high explosive, she was one of the most distinguished dancers of her day.

"She danced in the Quadrille: young and girlish, the more provocative because she played as a prude, with an assumed modesty . . . she was altogether adorable and excitable, morbid and sombre, biting and stinging; a creature of cruel moods . . ."   (Arthur Symons)

LOIE FULLER, an American dancer who invented a "serpentine and luminous" dance, in which she appeared swathed in veils, to perform in the beam of a colored spot-light.

LA GOULUE ("the Glutton"). (Her real name was Louise Weber), the leader of the *quadrille naturaliste* at the Moulin-Rouge and for several years the toast of Paris. Born in 1870, this "Circe of the can-can" led a vivacious career, as dancer, lion-tamer, laundress, finally to die in 1928 in abject poverty.

"La Goulue was a strange and tall girl, with a vampire's face, the profile of a bird of prey, a tortured mouth and metallic eyes; who danced always with definite gestures . . ."
          (Arthur Symons)

GRILLE-D'ÉGOUT ("Sewer Grating"). She earned her pretty name from eating and drinking everything in sight and because she had a large set of teeth. She belonged to the *quadrille quartette*.

IDA HEATH, a forgotten English dancer.

LA MACARONA, a dancer "famous for her effrontery" and her psyche of flaming hair.

* From the catalog published December 23, 1930, by the Art Institute of Chicago.

Cléo de Mérode, of the Paris opera, excelled in "the elaborate and picturesque Faust ballet." She made an American début in 1897, and was much painted as one of the beauties of her day.

May Milton, an English dancer who had a vogue in Paris in the late 'nineties.

"Her pale, almost clown-like face reminded one of a bull-dog and had nothing in it to hold one's attention, but her litheness, her wholly English enthusiasm for dancing . . . were a sort of revelation.
(Maurice Joyant)

Nini-Patte-en-l'Air ("Nini with the Hoof in the Air") another of the *quadrille*. She died a death—many might think enviable—from drinking two quarts of champagne.

"She was not young, she was not pretty, she was thin, short of stature, dark with heavy eyebrows, coarse, irregular features . . . all her extravagances were perfectly deliberate . . . it was with a sort of 'learned fury' that she danced; and she had a particular trick—the origin of her nickname—a particular quiver of the foot as the leg is held rigid in the air—which was her sign and signature."
(Arthur Symons)

Julia Subra, a Parisian ballet-dancer connected with the *Conservatoire National de Danse*.

Valentin le Desossé ("the Disjointed"), the partner of La Goulue in the waltz. He took his title from an extraordinary suppleness of limb.

"He certainly deserved his name, for he danced with an amazing dexterity, his thin legs defied caricature; and he, like the others, rarely lost his rhythm."
(Arthur Symons)

"There was an air of tragedy about his tall, famished figure, his gaunt face and lank hair; he had the mummified appearance of great age, and yet he danced with the ease of youth. They said he came of a distinguished family, that he himself had some intellectual attainments."
(M. Willson Disher)

SINGERS

Madame Abdala, a singer who had a successful début in Marseilles in 1891. She came to Paris the following year and after a short engagement at the *Ambassadeurs*, entered La Scala.

Émilienne d'Alençon, a favorite of the Paris music-halls.

Numa Auguez, singer at the Opera in Paris, who achieved a great reputation.

May Belfort, a singer of Irish origin, who performed in London music-halls about 1890. In 1895 she made her debut in Paris, at the *Cabaret des Décadents;* appearing also at the *Eden-Concert,* at the *Jardin de Paris,* and at the *Olympia.* Dressed as a baby and carrying a black kitten, she came on the scene to lisp the words of her favorite song:

> "I have a little cat
> I'm very fond of that."

Paula Brébion, a singer in the *café-concert*, whose powerful voice carried her as far as La Scala.

Aristide Bruant, founder of the *Cabaret Mirliton* at 84 Boulevard Rochechouart, which opened in 1885 and soon became the rage of Paris. Bruant appeared nightly wearing a "black velvet loose coat and trousers, black top-boots, a red shirt, collar and black scarf," singing his own sentimental ballads of love and misery, shrewdly composed in the *argot* of the boulevards.

In 1893 and 1894 he appeared at the *Ambassadeurs* and at the *Eldorado*.

"He was clean-shaven, with a powerful face, hair brushed back, fine features, a certain dignity and occasionally a genial smile. He sang his own songs to his own music, in a loud and monotonous voice and without emphasis, always walking to and fro." (Arthur Symons)

Rose Caron, a famous member of the Paris Opera. Sang rôles of Brunnhilda, Marguerite, Salammbô and Elsa.

Pierre Ducarre, director of the *Concert des Ambassadeurs*, was born in Châteauneuf-sur-Sornin in 1830. He came to Paris in 1848 where he served as a waiter in the *Café Turc*. Later he founded the *Café des Porcherons*, which he left in 1867 to take over the *Concert des Ambassadeurs*, which under his direction became world renowned.

Juliette Joséphine Girad, lyric singer, who is remembered for her rôles in "Cloches de Corneville," "Madame Favart," etc.

Yvette Guilbert, the greatest of the music-hall singers; "Yvette is the one woman of genius," writes Arthur Symons, "among many notable and remarkable persons of talent." Born in 1868, the daughter of an inconspicuous draper, she rose rapidly to fame, conquering one music-hall after another. Her range was remarkable; every type of song, tragic, humorous, pathetic or malicious; in each she was superlative.

"No, she isn't beautiful, a flat face, a nose that has nothing Greek in it, eyes with a wild light in them, eyelids rather Satanical, a heap of reddish hair; flat breasts: that's the woman." (Goncourt)

"Yvette begins to sing and immediately the gay world that you see across the smoke of your cigarette seems to unmask itself, becomes too suddenly serious, tragic, a piece of real existence." (Arthur Symons)

Mary Hamilton, a café-singer who made a reputation for herself in male impersonation.

Anna Held, the "inimitable Anna," was born in Paris and spent most of her life singing in various music-halls, where she was famous for her English and American songs. She died in New York in 1918.

Cecy Loftus (Marie Cecilia M'Carthy), born in Glasgow in 1876. First appeared as a mimic in the Oxford Music Hall in 1893. Played in London and later in America, with E. H. Sothern and Modjeska. Still acting on Broadway.

Polaire (Émilie Zouzée), born in Algiers in 1879. After singing at the *Ambassadeurs*, she performed at many theaters in Paris, notably the *Variétés* and the *Renaissance*.

Polin, a singer who excelled in racy imitations. Later sang in "Champignol malgré Lui," and "Chéri."

ACTORS AND ACTRESSES

Antoine, a theatrical manager and actor, born in Limoges in 1851. In 1887 he founded the *Théâtre Libre*. Became Co-director of the *Odéon* in 1896 and Director in 1906.

"He was ugly, with no good features, no profile, a large nose, a receding chin, bright unflinching eyes, and a mobile, typical actor's face. He impressed me at once: he had enthusiasm, and he had judgment; he was vivid, impressionable, reflective." (Arthur Symons)

Baron (Louis Bouchenez). Born in 1838, he played at the *Variétés*, and the *Comédie*, his greatest success being the rôle of Baron Gros in "La Grande-Duchesse."

Bartet (Jeanne Julia Regnault), born in 1854. She made her début in 1872, and played at the Théâtre Français in 1879. Principle rôles: "L'Arlésienne," "L'Oncle Sam," and "Dora."

Marthe Brandès, an actress who played at the *Comédie*, 1893–1903. Acted in "Ruy-Blas," "Tartuffe," and in many modern plays. Left the theater in 1914.

Albert Brasseur, part-founder of the *Théâtre des Nouveautés*, and famous in his day.

Mlle. Cassive, a popular actress of the time. Triumphed in "La Dame de chez Maxim."

Coquelin, Aîné, one of the greatest actors of his period. During twenty-two years he created the leading parts in forty-four new plays. Toured Europe and America with Bernhardt, achieving his greatest personal success in "Cyrano de Bergerac," written for him by Rostand.

Félix Galipaux, actor and author of several volumes connected with the stage.

Firmin Gémier, actor and Director of the *Théâtre Antoine*.

Jeanne Granier, an actress who played in "Madame le Diable," "Mme. Satan," etc.

Lucien German Guitry (1860–1925); first appeared in "Camille." Bernhardt invited him to the *Théâtre de la Renaissance* where he made his great reputation.

23

Georges Guillaume Guy, an actor at the *Folies Dramatiques*, the *Nouveautés* and the *Variétés*.

Jane Hading, a popular actress of the *Odéon* and *Comédie*.

Judic (Mme. Anna Damiens), (1850–1911), an actress who made her début at the *Conservatoire* in 1867. She toured Europe and the United States and played with Bernhardt.

Eva Lavallière, an actress at the *Variétés*. Played in "Le Nouveau Jeu" (1898).

Marcelle Lender, a well-known actress and singer of the period, who played in "Mme. Satan," at the *Variétés* in 1893, and danced the bolero in Hervé's "Chilpéric," in 1896.

Aurélien Lugné-Poë, an actor-manager who founded the French school of modern drama.

Henry Mayer, musician and actor, played in vaudeville and at the *Odéon* and *Théâtre Libre* in many modern dramas.

Mounet-Sully (Jean Sully), (1841–1916), great tragedian at the *Théâtre Français*. Chief rôles: "Le Cid," "Hamlet," "Oedipus Rex," etc.

Réjane (1857–1920), actress and *directrice* of the *Théâtre Réjane*. Played in "Lysistrata," "Sapho," and "The Doll's House."

FRIENDS

Maxime Dethomas, born 1867. The artist who supervised the decorating of the *Théâtre National de l'Opéra*, Paris.

Désiré Dihau (1825–1909), musician and composer and cousin of Toulouse-Lautrec. He left numerous compositions, some of them with covers by the artist.

The Natansons, Alexandre and Thadée, two brothers who founded the *Revue Blanche*, which published Lautrec. With their wives, they created a salon, where one met the literary and artistic public of Paris. Lautrec painted them very often, sometimes at Villeneuve-sur-Yonne.

Paul Sescau, friend and photographer. Lautrec was passionately interested in cameras, and made a poster for Sescau.

Dr. Tapié de Céleyran, cousin and companion of Lautrec. He was connected with the *Hôpital International*.

ODILON REDON

Odilon Redon. Born at Bordeaux, April 20, 1840. Began to draw at the age of ten. Early interest in Delacroix. Failure at the Beaux Arts. Entered Atelier Gérôme. Dissatisfied in his work. 1856, Tried architecture and sculpture. Began a false Barbizon style under the influence of Corot and Chintreuil. Interest in botany through Armand Clavaud. 1863, Learned lithography and etching from Rudolphe Bresdin. 1866, The beginning of the strong mystical element in his work. 1879, Publication of the first collection of lithographs *Dans le Rêve* under the technical help of Fantin-Latour. 1899, Turned to working in oil, pastel, and watercolor. Died July 6, 1916.

*67 ANDROMEDA†

Oil

Collection C. W. Kraushaar, New York

68 ANDROMEDA

Oil

Collection Martin A. Ryerson, Chicago

69 BERNADETTE L'ARCHE

Collection Jacques Seligmann and Company, New York and Paris

*70 THE BIRTH OF VENUS

Oil

Collection Dr. B. D. Saklatwalla, Crafton, Pennsylvania

71 BOUQUET OF FLOWERS

Oil

Collection Mr. and Mrs. Samuel A. Lewisohn, New York

72 BUTTERFLIES

Watercolor
Collection James W. Barney, New York
Courtesy The Art Museum of Yale University

73 THE CAT

Oil

Collection Martin A. Ryerson, Chicago

† Because of the difficulty in definitely ascribing dates to many of Redon's paintings, his works are here alphabetically listed. The medium is pastel unless otherwise indicated. No attempt has been made to show the lithographs of Redon.

74 THE CHILD
Collection Martin A. Ryerson, Chicago

75 CHRIST
Watercolor
Collection Mrs. F. R. Lillie, Chicago

*76 APPARITION
Oil
Collection Dr. W. R. Valentiner, Detroit

*77 THE CROWN
Collection Mrs. C. J. Martin, Minneapolis

78 DANTE AND BEATRICE
Oil
Collection Dr. W. R. Valentiner, Detroit

*79 DANTESQUE VISION
Watercolor
Collection John A. Holabird, Chicago

80 DECORATIVE PANEL
Oil
Collection Mrs. John Alden Carpenter, Chicago

*81 DREAM OF THE BUTTERFLIES
Oil
Collection The Detroit Institute of Arts, Detroit

82 DREAM SHADOWS (HEAD OF GIRL)
Collection Mr. and Mrs. Samuel A. Lewisohn, New York

The following is a notation by Redon on the constitution of "une bonne palette." Blanc de plomb, jaune Mars, ocre jaune, jaune antimoine, orange Mars, Sienne brûlée, rose Mars, ocre rouge, laque fine, violet de cobalt, bleu d'outremer, vert émeraude, terre verte, terre d'ombre naturelle, noire de pêche, jaune de Naples et vermillon, sans mélange aucun de blanc de plomb.

From André Mellerio, *Odilon Redon*, Paris, 1923, p. 138.

83 DUTCH GIRLS
Collection John A. Holabird, Chicago

84 ETRUSCAN VASE
Private Collection, New York

85 EVOCATION OF THE BUTTERFLIES
Collection The Detroit Institute of Arts, Detroit

86 FANTASTIC ORCHID
Watercolor
Collection Hardinge Scholle, New York

87 FLOWERS
Oil
Collection Dr. B. D. Saklatwalla, Crafton, Pennsylvania

88 FLOWERS AND BUTTERFLIES
Collection Mrs. Cornelius N. Bliss, Jr., New York

89 HEAD IN PROFILE
Drawing
Collection Alexander M. Bing, New York

90 HEAD OF CHRIST
Watercolor
Collection Dr. B. D. Saklatwalla, Crafton, Pennsylvania

*91 HEAD WITH FLOWERS
Oil
Collection M. B. Sanders, Jr., New York

*92 LANDSCAPE
Oil
Collection Mrs. Diodata O'Toole, New York

93 ORGANIC MATTER
Watercolor
Private Collection, New York

94 PANDORA
Oil
Collection Alexander M. Bing, New York

*95 PEGASUS
Drawing
Collection Philip Hofer, New York

96 POT OF GERANIUMS
Oil
Collection Mr. and Mrs. Ralph M. Coe, Cleveland

*97 PROFILE AND FLOWERS
Collection Jacques Seligmann and Company, New York and Paris

98 ROGER AND ANGELICA
Private Collection, New York

99 SILENCE
Oil
Private Collection, New York

*100 SPRING
Oil
Collection The Worcester Art Museum, Worcester

101 VASE OF ANEMONES
Collection Thomas Cochran, New York

102 VASE OF FLOWERS
Collection Mrs. Cornelius N. Bliss, Jr., New York

103 VASE OF FLOWERS
Collection Albert E. McVitty, Bryn Mawr, Pennsylvania

*104 THE VIRGIN

    Oil

    Collection James W. Barney, New York

    Courtesy The Art Museum of Yale University

105 WOMAN AMONG FLOWERS

    Collection Martin A. Ryerson, Chicago

ILLUSTRATIONS

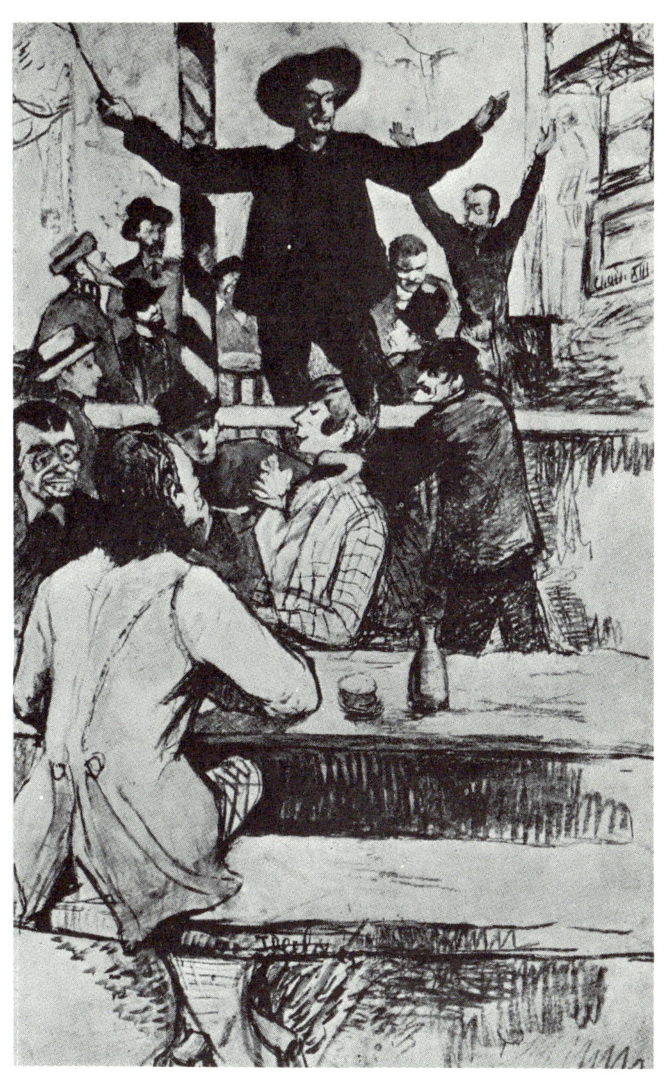

The Louis XIII Chair at Bruant's Cabaret (1886)
Oil on cardboard mounted on canvas, 20½ x 31 inches
Collection Messrs. Durand-Ruel, New York and Paris

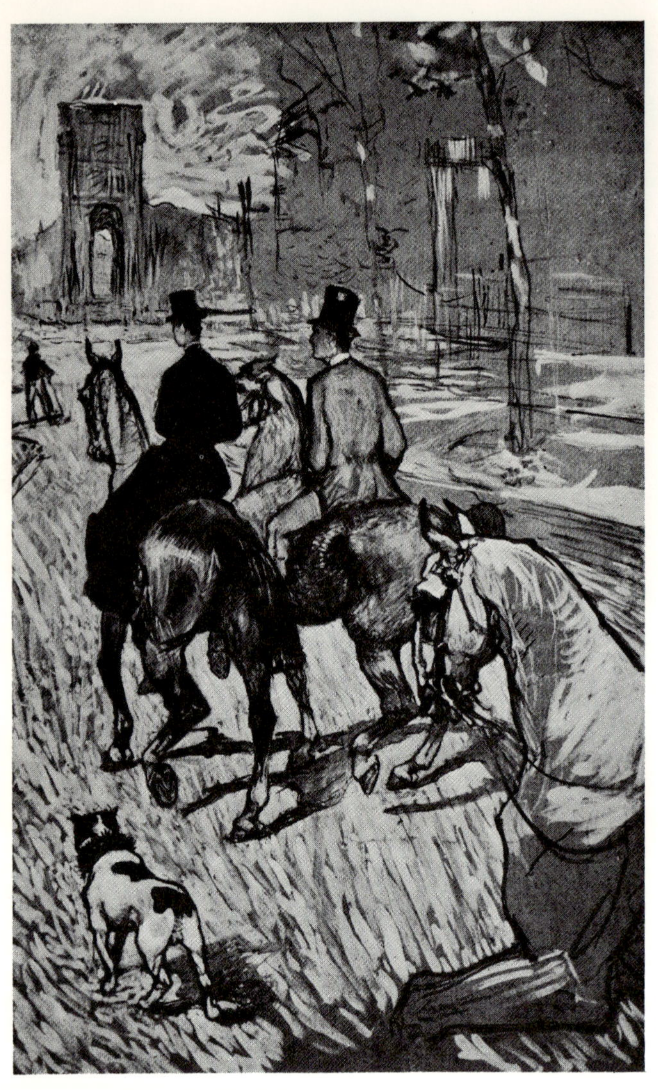

5 LAUTREC
RIDERS ON THEIR WAY TO THE BOIS DE BOULOGNE (1888)
Black and white on cardboard, 33¼ x 19¾ inches
Collection Adolph Lewisohn, New York

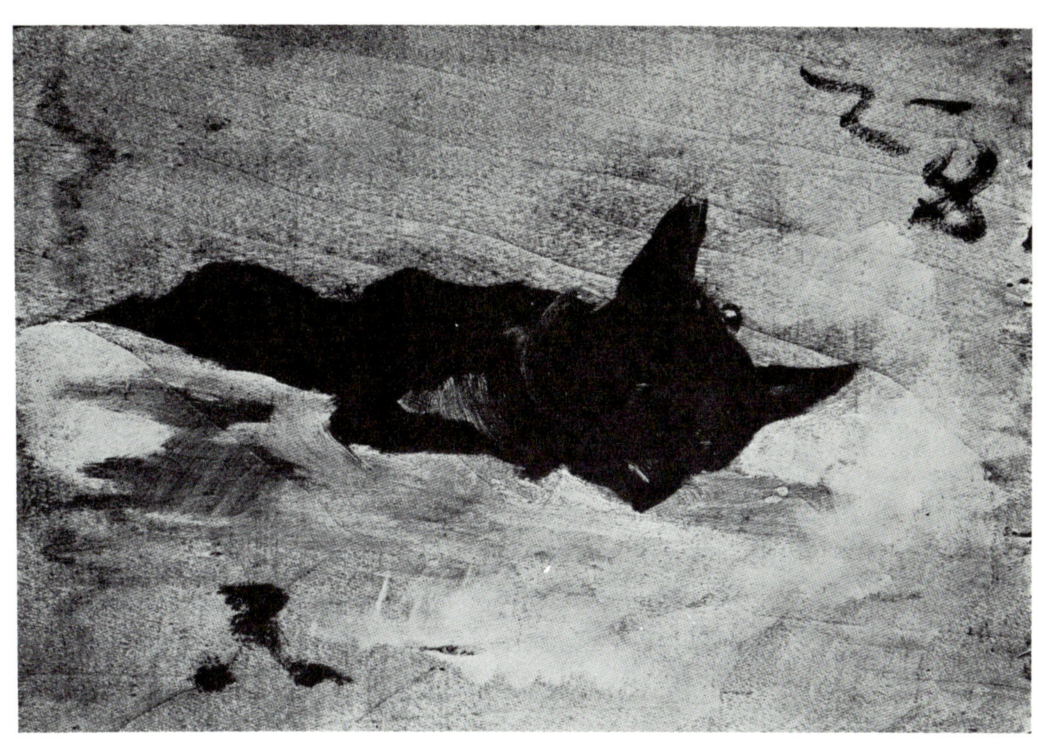

LITTLE DOG (1888). *Oil on wood, 6¼ x 9⅛ inches*
Collection William Preston Harrison Los Angeles

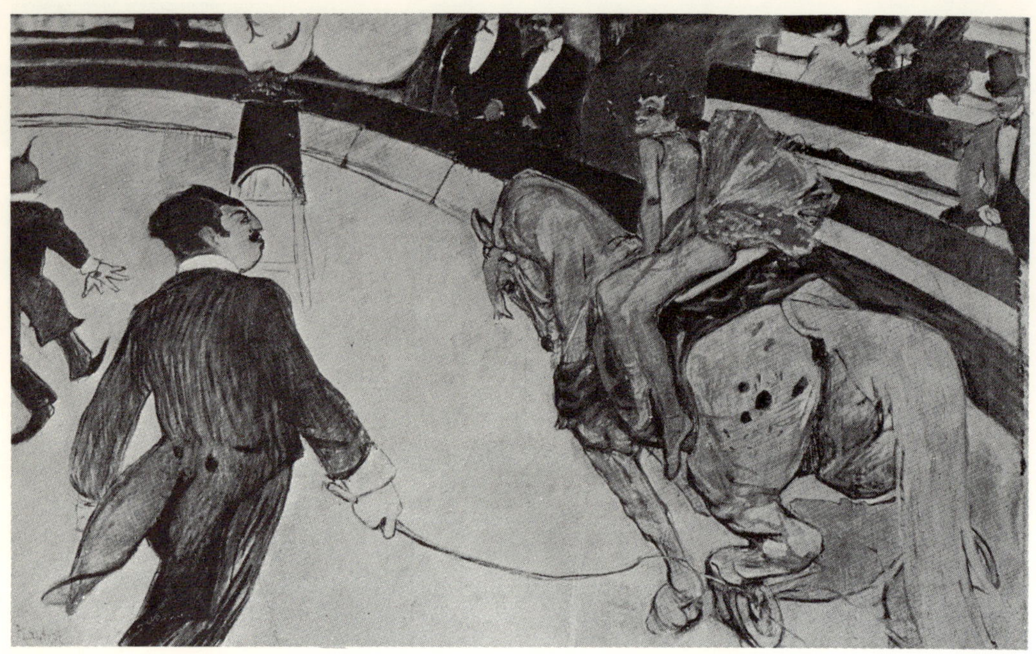

7 LAUTREC

At the Circus Fernando. The Ring Master (1888). *Oil on canvas, 38¾ x 63½ inches*
Collection The Art Institute of Chicago (Joseph Winterbotham Collection)

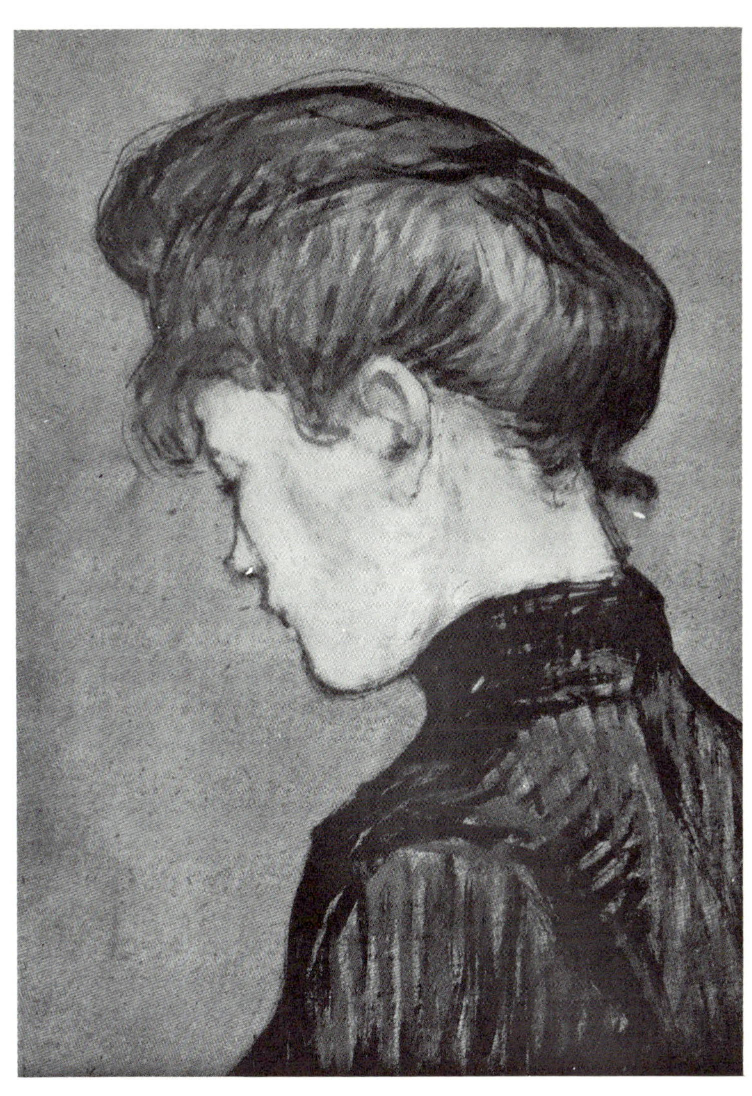

LAUTREC 8
HEAD OF A WOMAN. *Oil on cardboard, 13 ½ x 27 inches*
Collection Paul Lamb, Cleveland

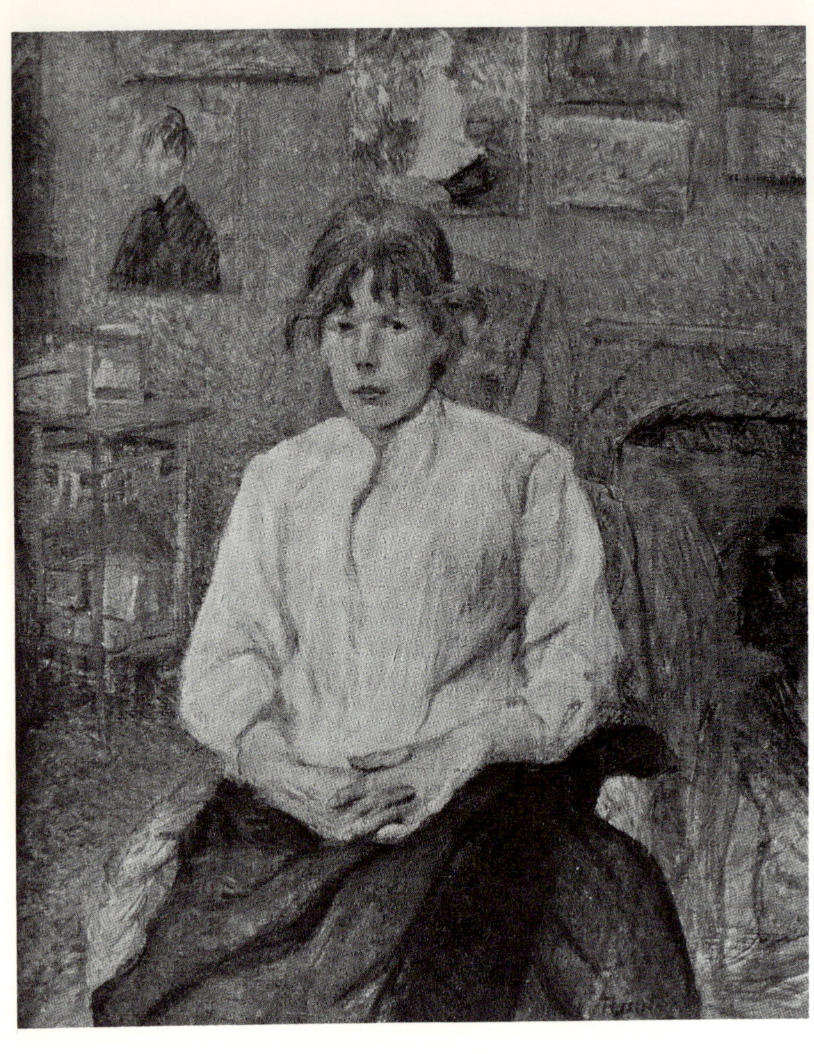

9 LAUTREC
WOMAN IN A STUDIO. *Oil on canvas, 22 x 18 inches*
Collection John T. Spaulding, Boston

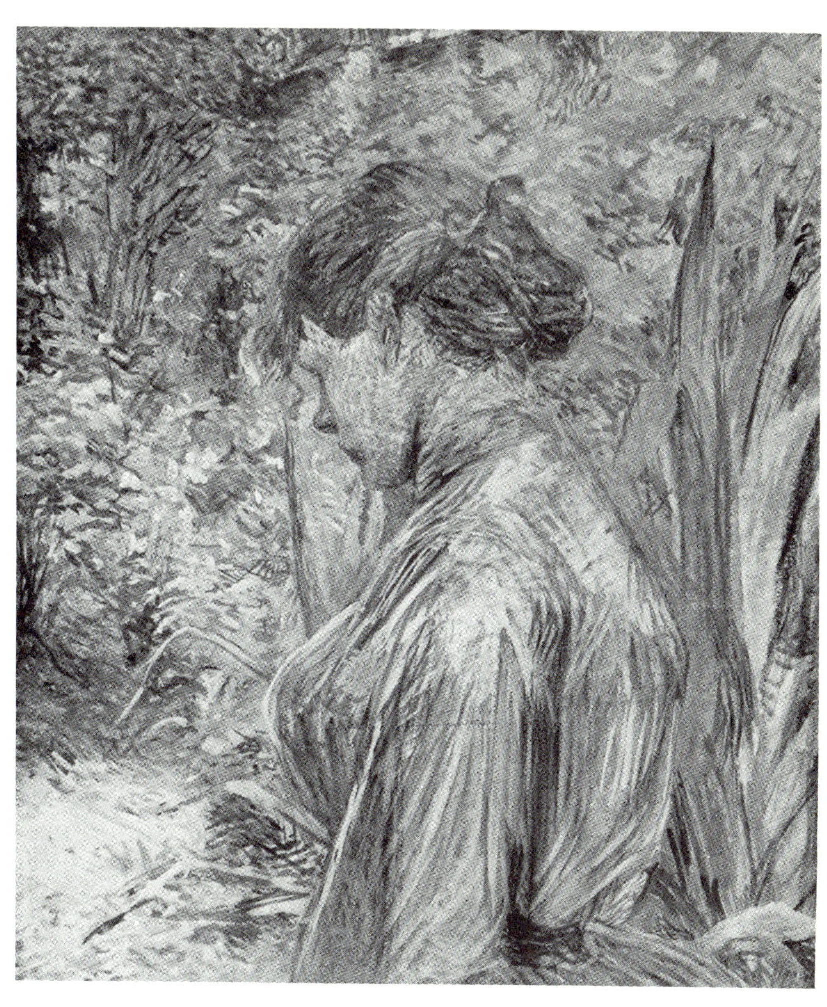

LAUTREC 10

RUSSIAN WOMAN (1889). *Oil on cardboard, 28 x 23 inches*
Collection The Albright Art Gallery, Buffalo

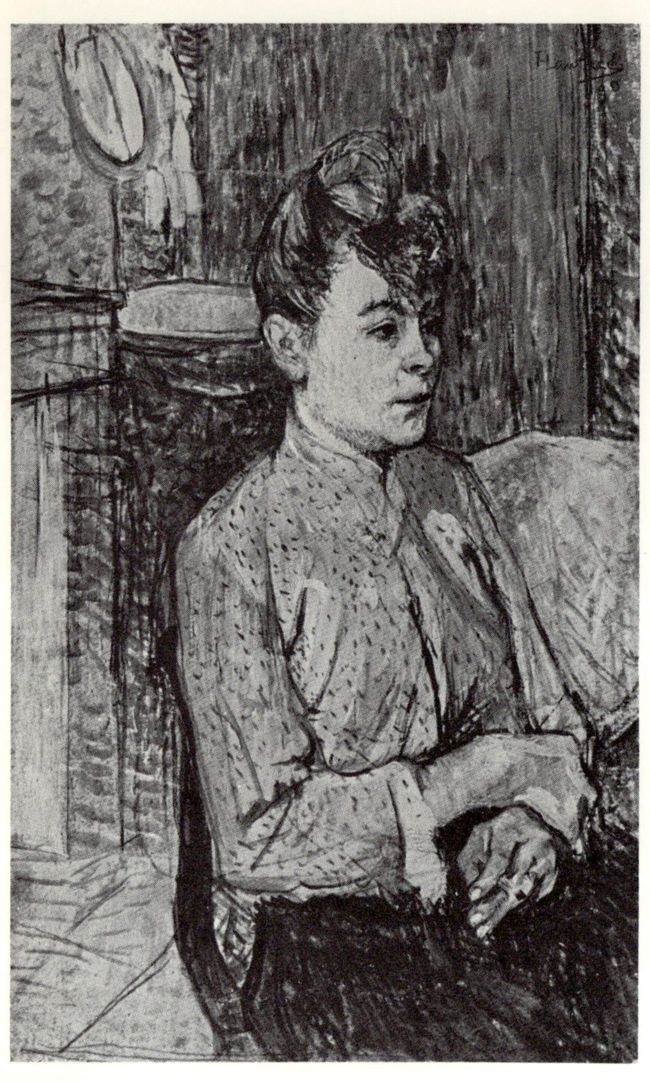

12 LAUTREC

Woman Smoking A Cigarette (1890). *Oil on cardboard,* 18½ x 11¾ *inches*
Collection The Brooklyn Museum

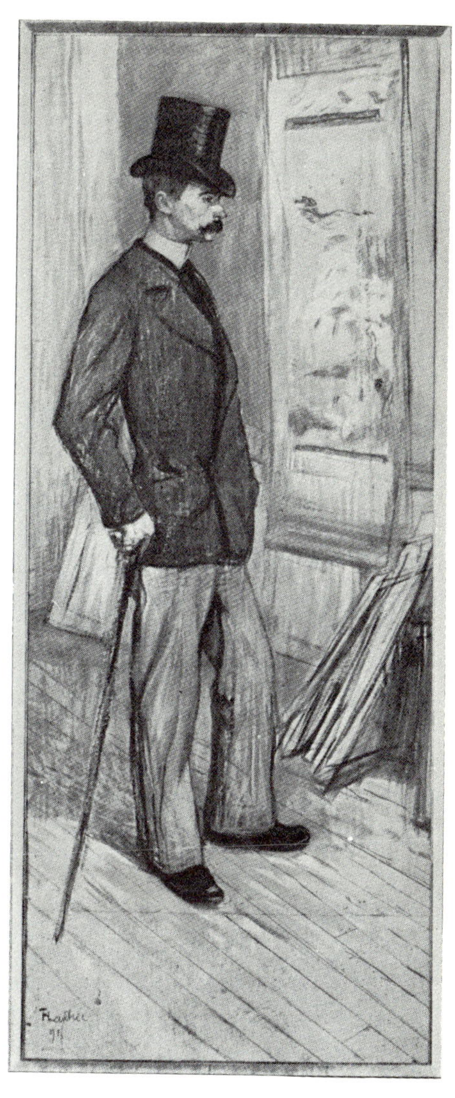

LAUTREC 13

PORTRAIT OF PAUL SESCAU (1891). *Oil on paper, 39½ x 20¾ inches*
Collection The Brooklyn Museum

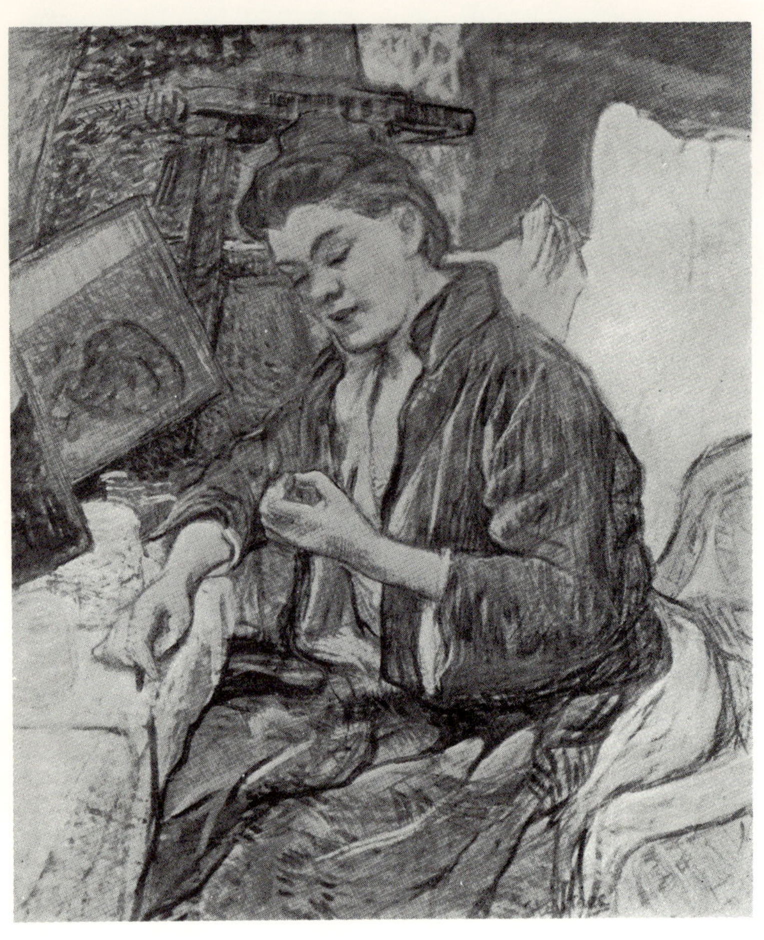

15 LAUTREC

THE TOILETTE (1891). *Oil on cardboard, 28¾ x 25½ inches*
Collection Mr. and Mrs. Cornelius J. Sullivan, New York

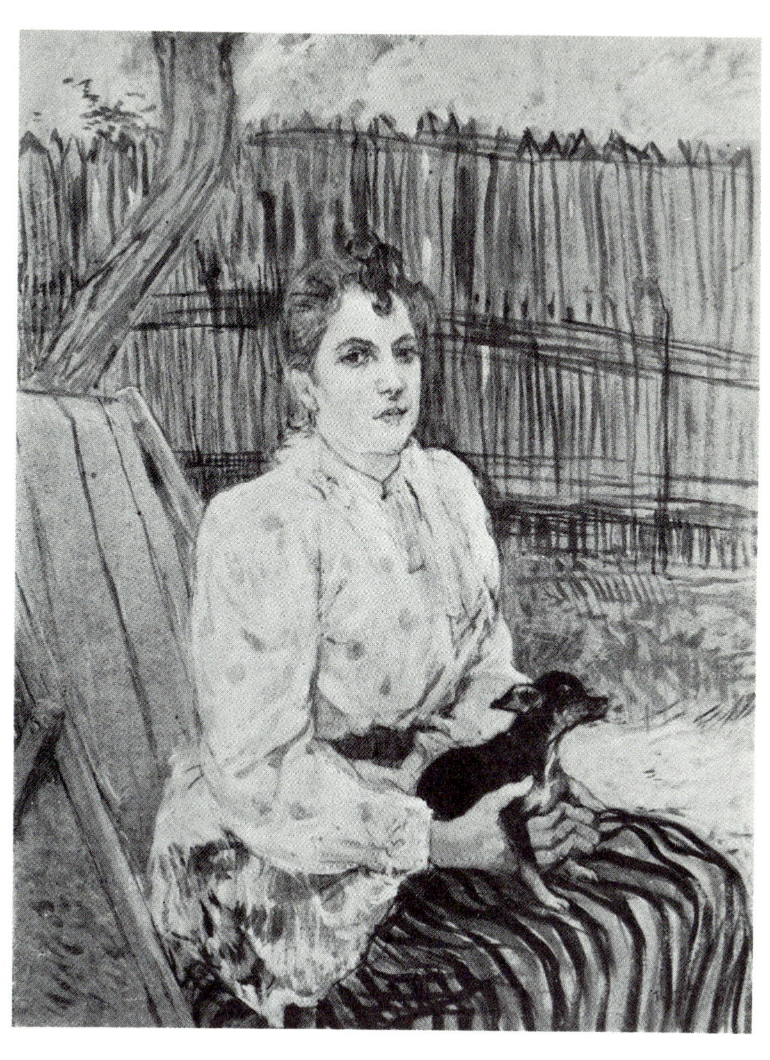

LADY WITH A DOG. *Oil on cardboard, 29 x 22½ inches*
Collection Gerald Brooks, New York

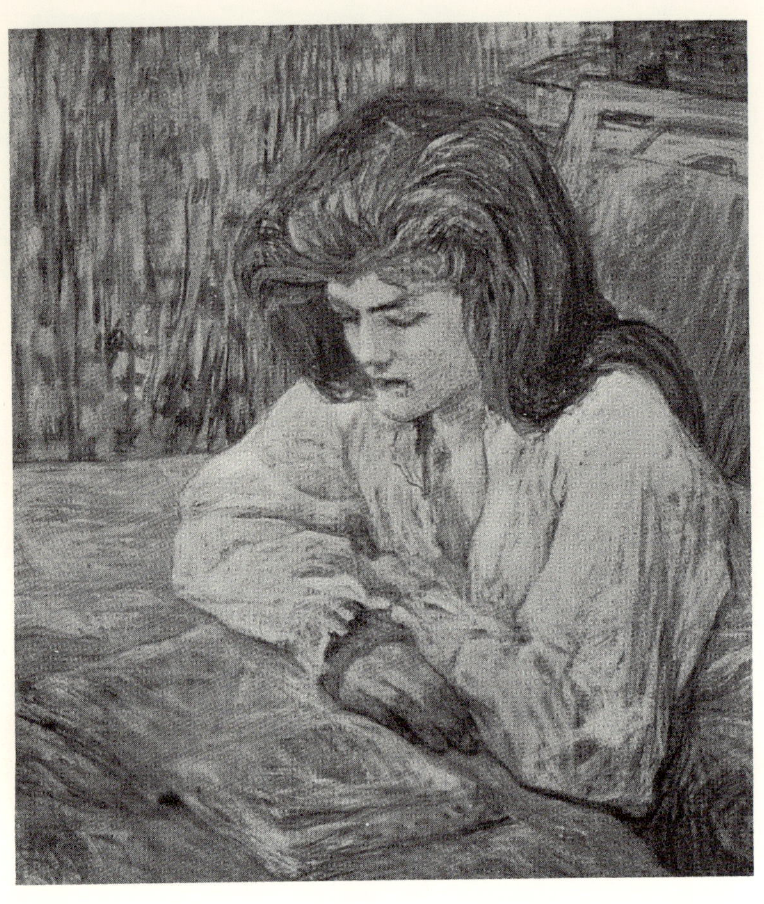

17 LAUTREC
READING. *Oil on cardboard, 27 x 23 ½ inches*
Collection Adolph Lewisohn, New York

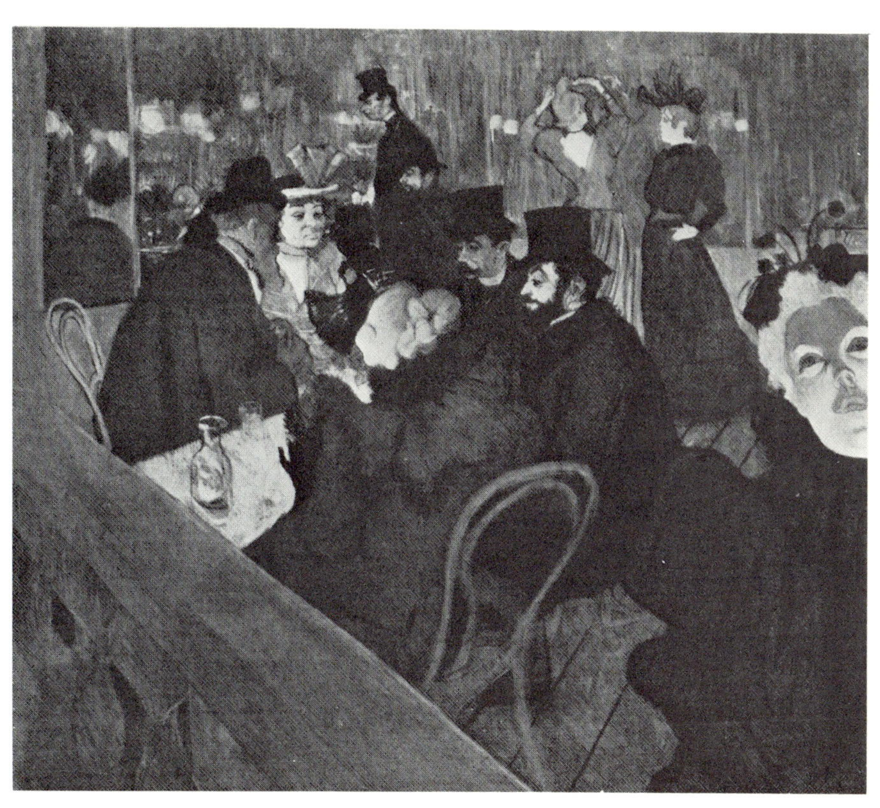

AT THE MOULIN-ROUGE (1892). *Oil on canvas,* 55¼ x 47¼ *inches*
The Art Institute of Chicago, The Birch-Bartlett Collection

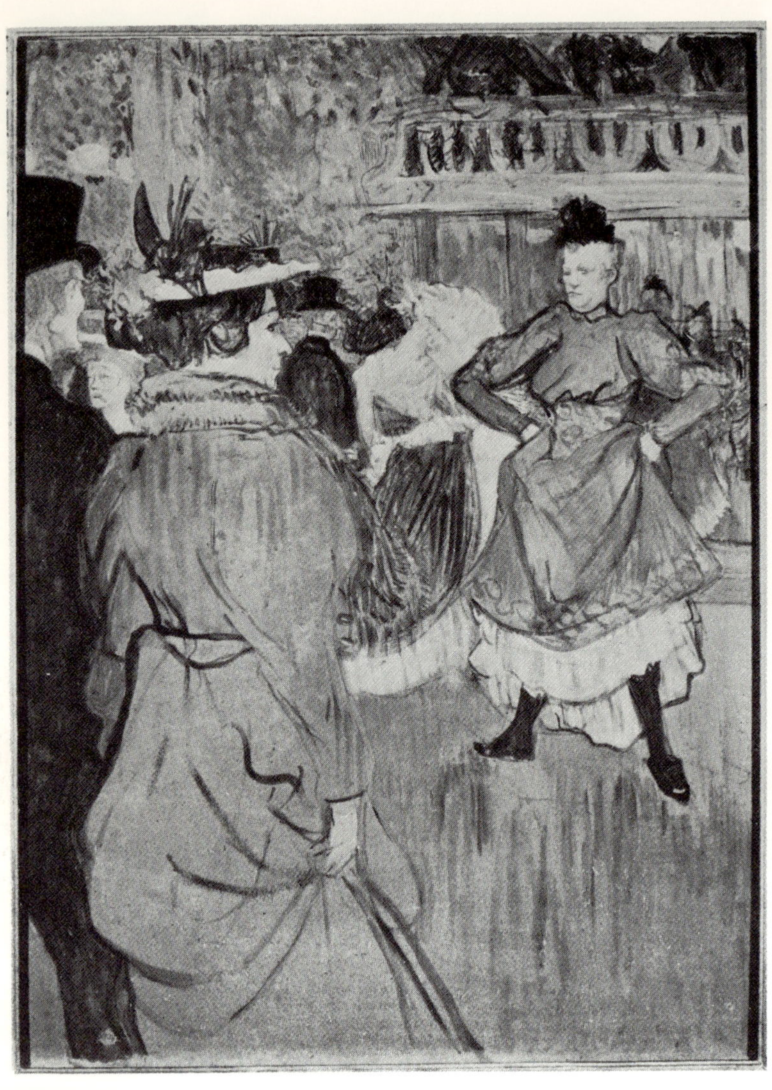

20 LAUTREC

The Quadrille at the Moulin-Rouge (1892). *Pastel on cardboard, 31 ½ x 23¾ inches*
The Chester Dale Collection, New York

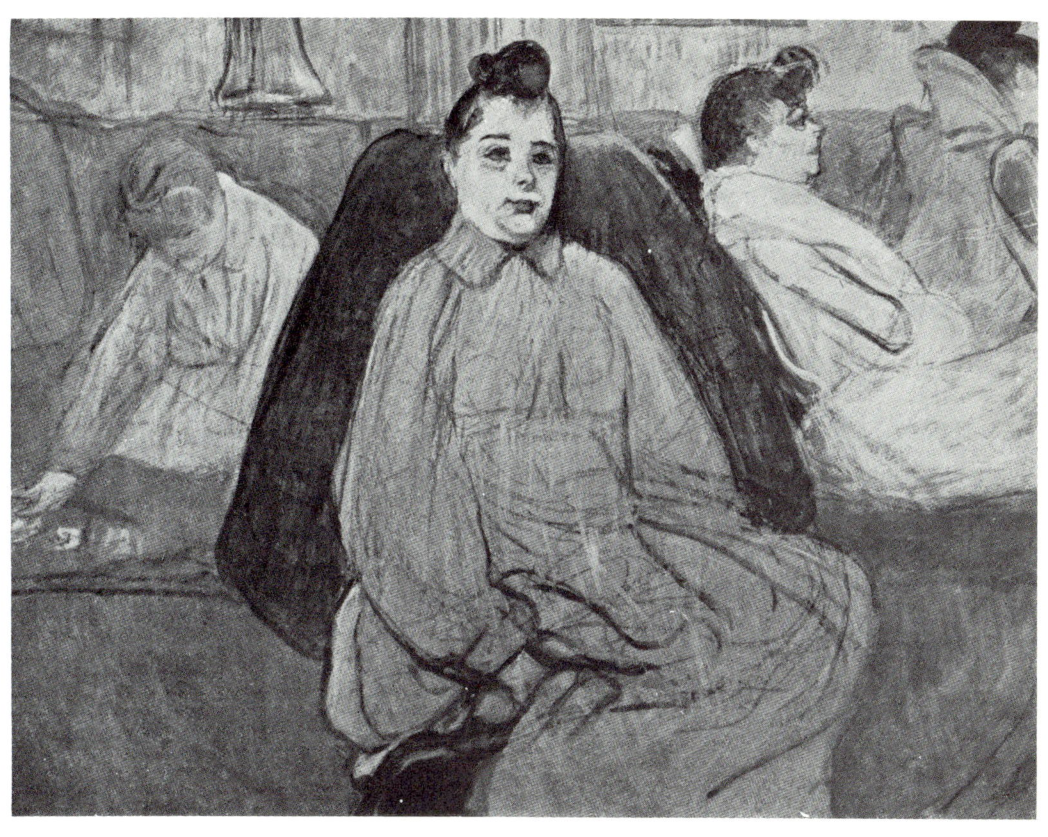

THE DIVAN (1893). *Oil on cardboard, 21⅛ x 27¼ inches*
Collection Wildenstein and Company, New York and Paris

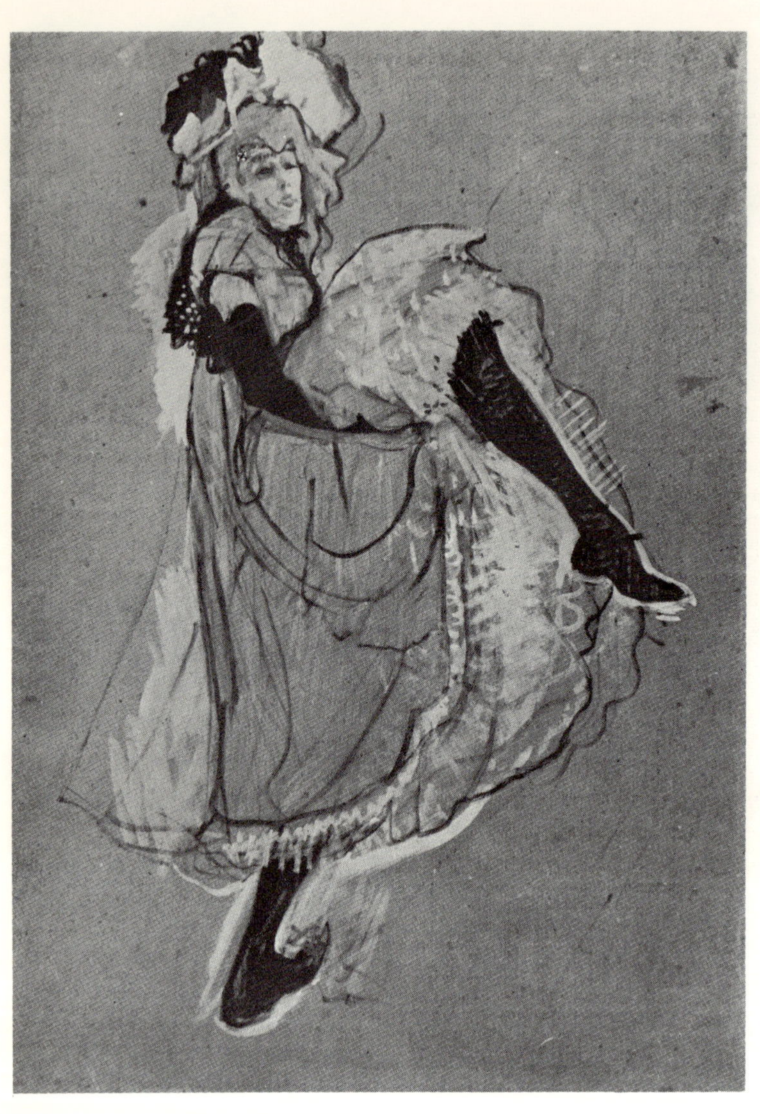

22 LAUTREC

JANE AVRIL DANCING (1893). *Oil on cardboard, 39¾ x 29 inches*
Collection Wildenstein and Company, New York and Paris

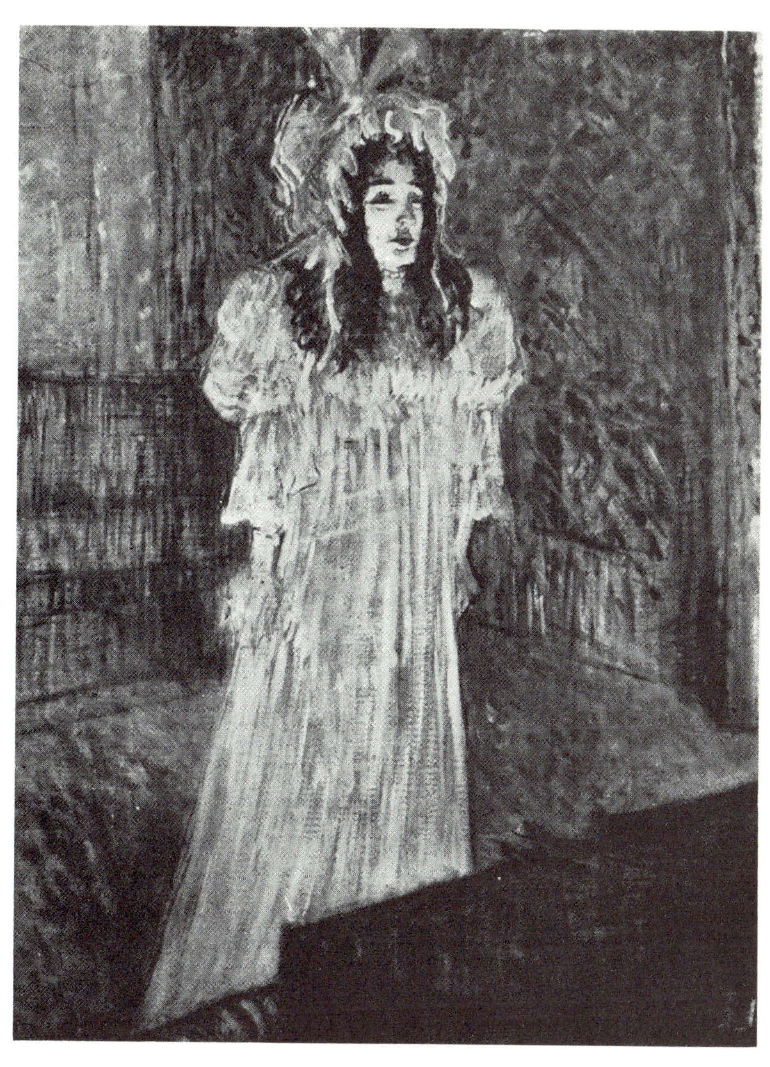

MISS MAY BELFORT (1895). *Oil on cardboard, 24½ x 19 inches*
Private Collection, New York

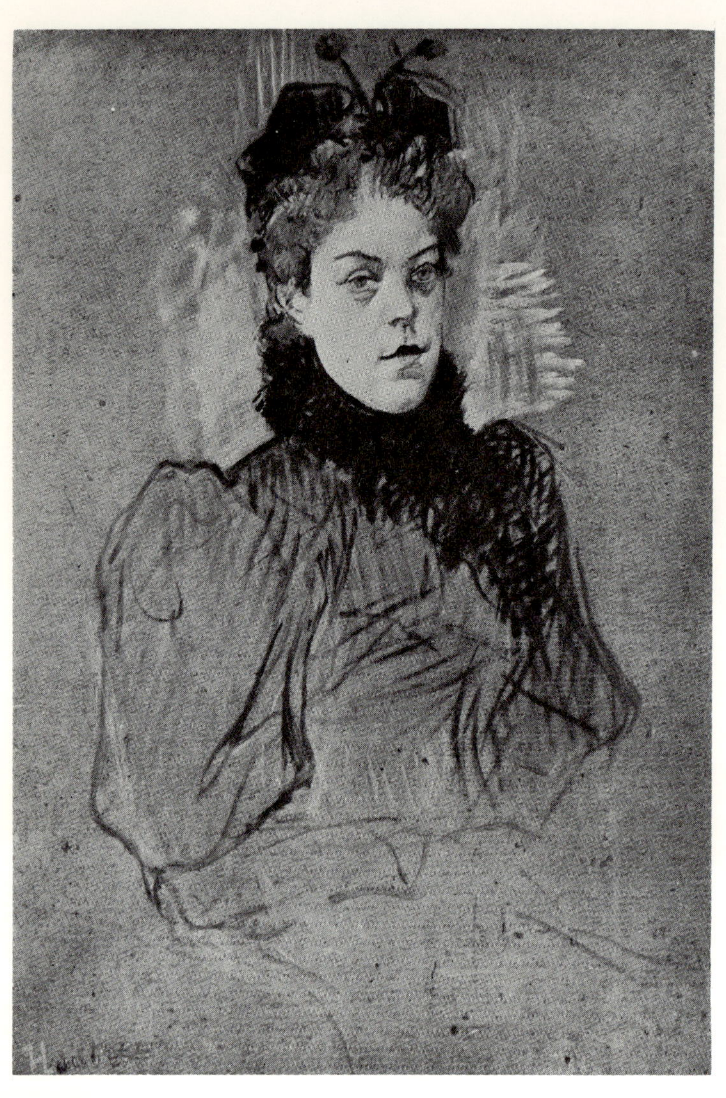

24 LAUTRIC

PORTRAIT OF MAY MILTON (1895). *Oil on cardboard, 25 ½ x 18¾ inches*
Collection Walter S. Brewster, Chicago

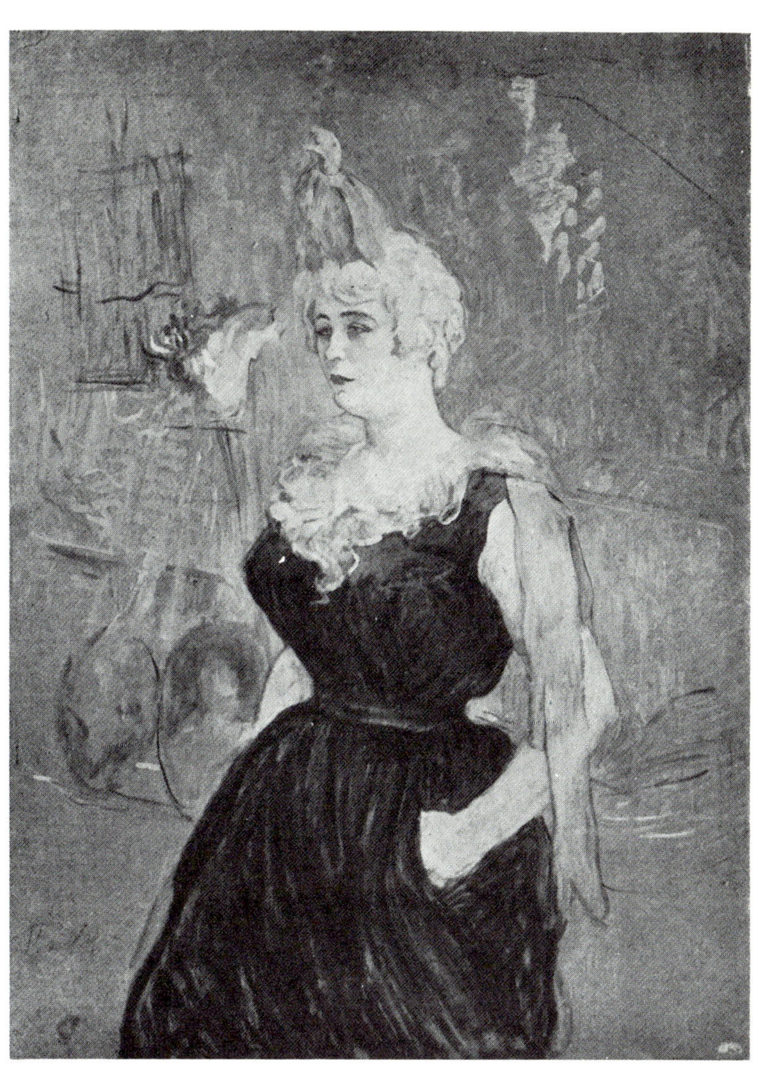

LAUTREC 25

La Clowness Cha-U-Kao (1895). *Oil on cardboard, 32 x 23 ½ inches*
Collection Frank H. Ginn, Cleveland

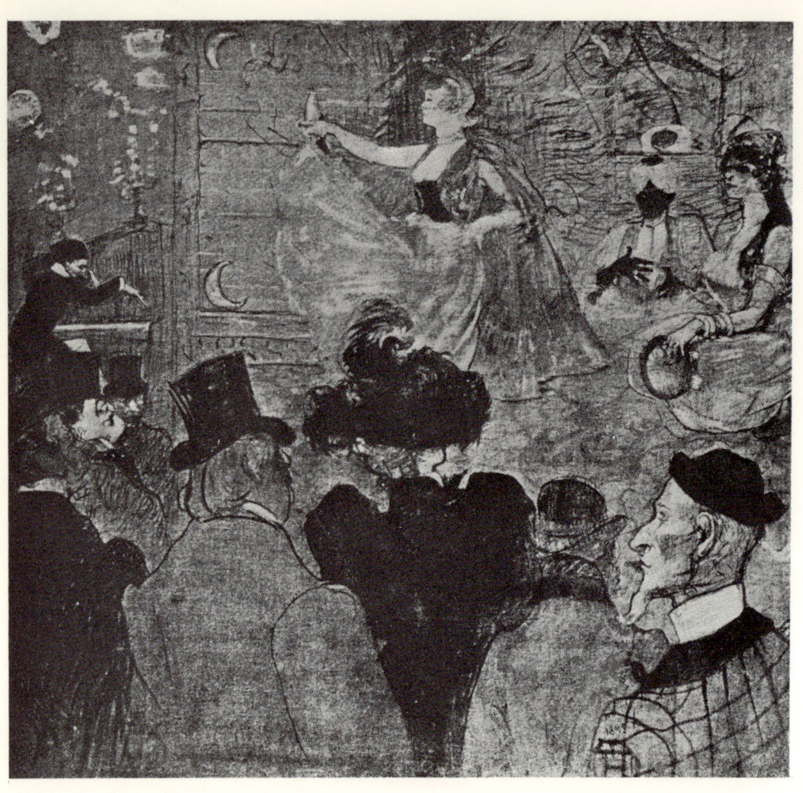

26 LAUTREC

The Moorish Dance or "Les Almées" (1895). Oil on canvas, 118⅛ x 118⅛ inches
Collection The Louvre Museum, Paris

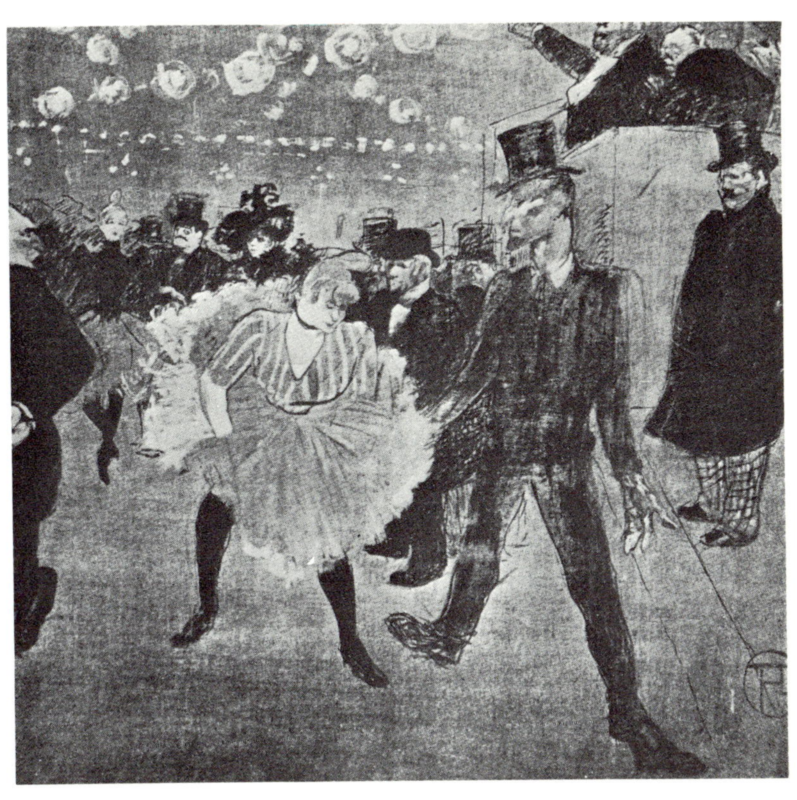

The Dance at the Moulin-Rouge (1895). *Oil on canvas, 118⅛ x 118⅛ inches*
Collection The Louvre Museum, Paris

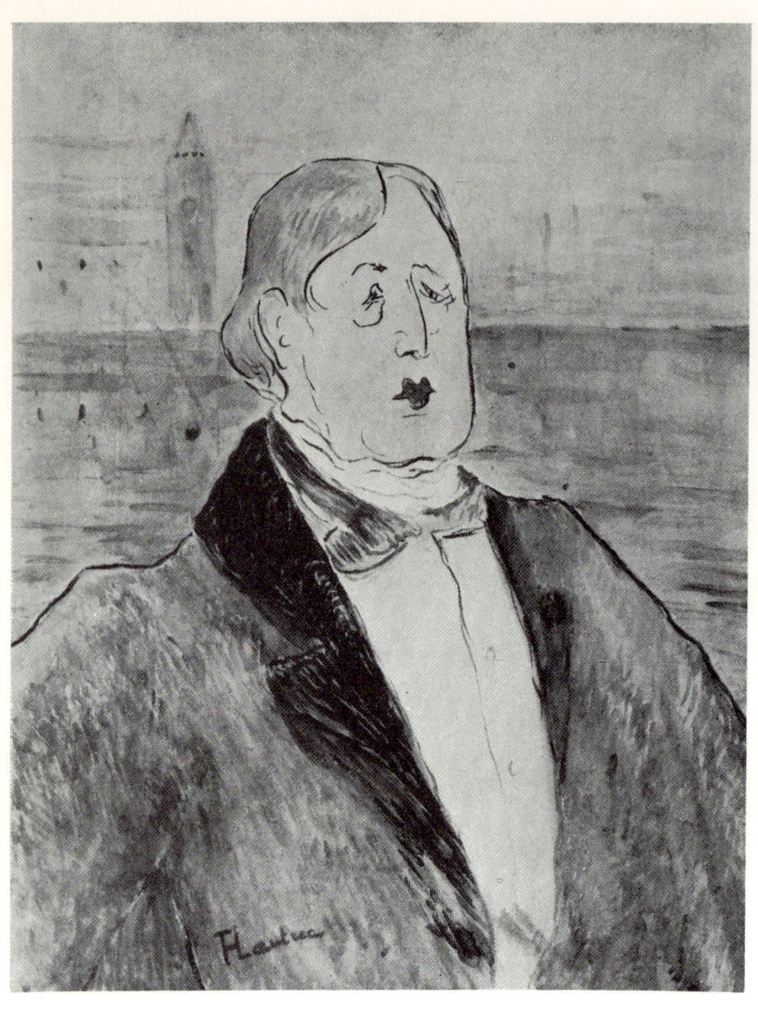

28 LAUTREC

PORTRAIT OF OSCAR WILDE (1895). *Watercolor on paper, 24 x 19½ inches*
Collection Messrs. Jacques Seligmann and Company, New York and Paris

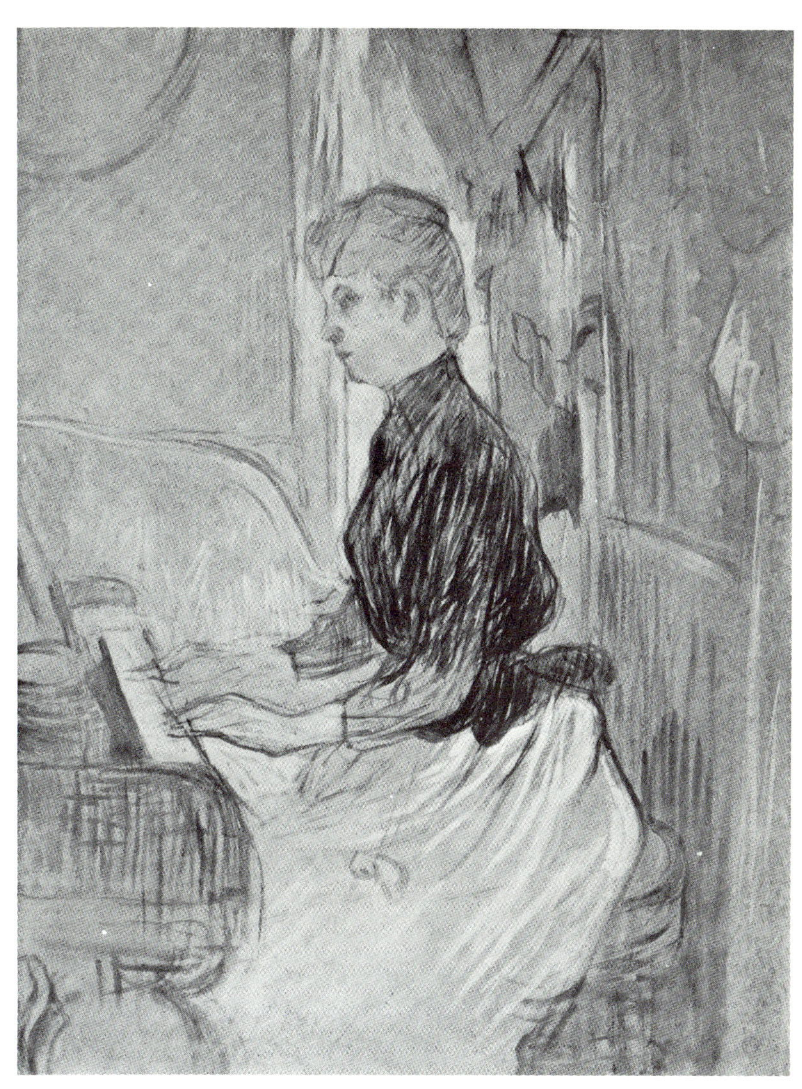

LADY AT THE PIANO (1896). *Oil on cardboard, 29½ x 23½ inches*
Private Collection Josef Stransky, New York

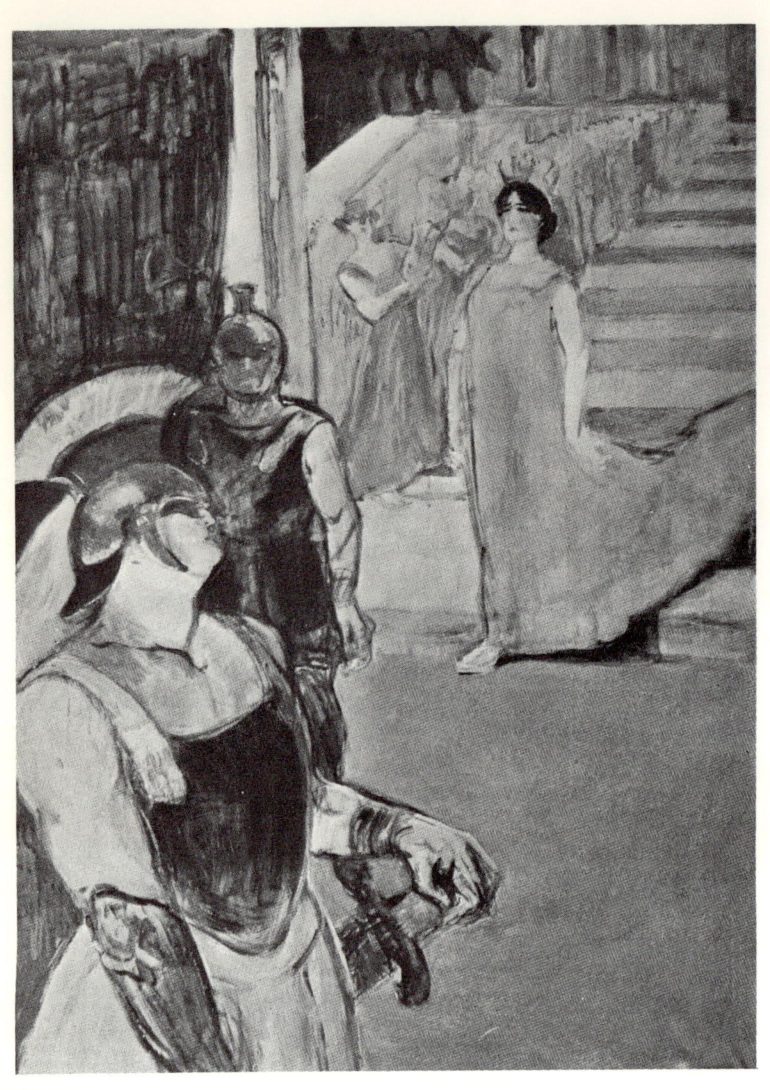

34 LAUTREC

Messalina (Bordeaux, 1900). *Oil on canvas, 39 x 28½ inches*
Collection Adolph Lewisohn, New York

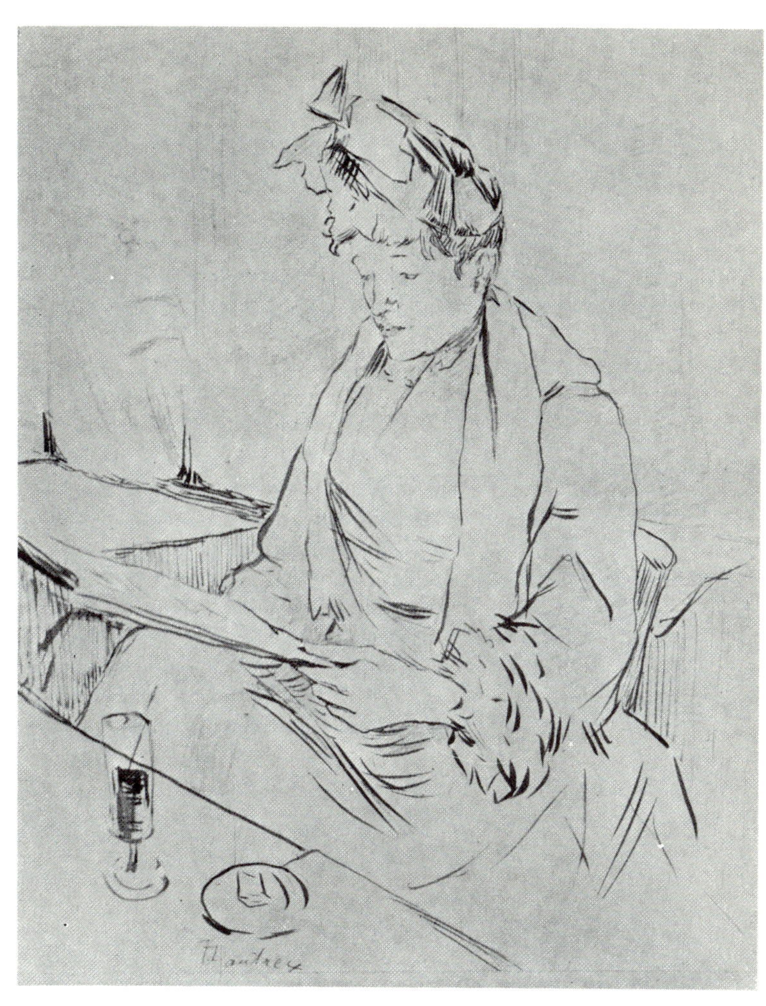

LAUTREC 36

Au Café. *Brush, ink and blue chalk on yellow paper, 26½ x 23¾ inches*
Collection John Nicholas Brown, Providence, Rhode Island

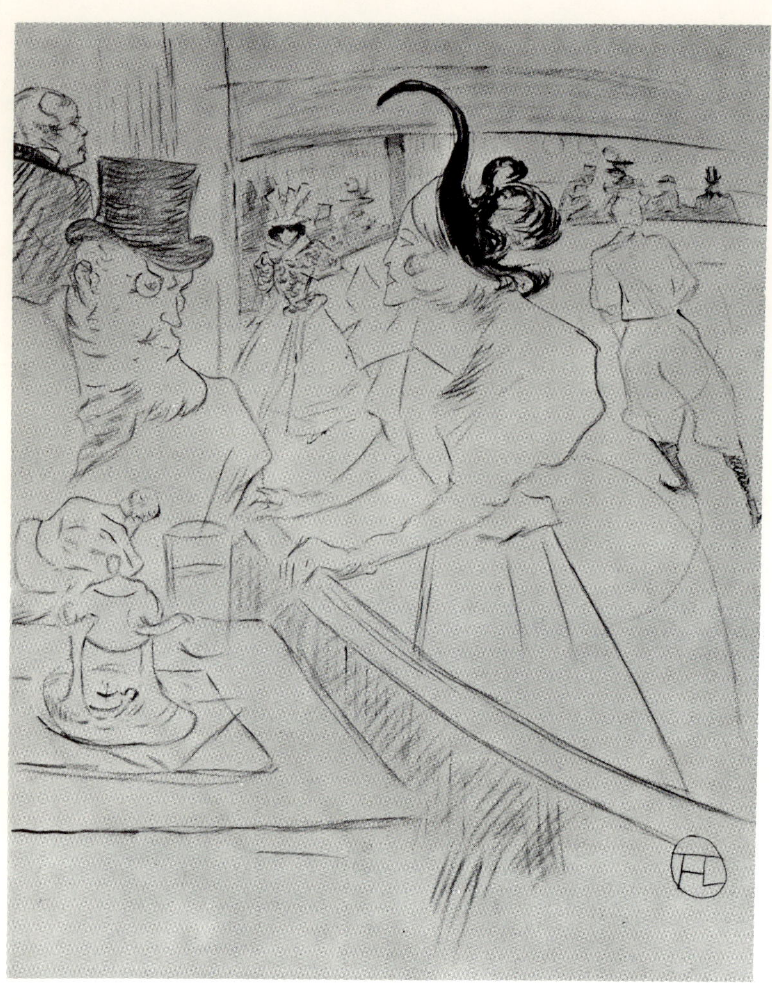

41 LAUTREC

SKATING: PROFESSIONAL BEAUTY (1896)

Drawing colored with gouache and crayon on paper, 25¾ x 20¾ inches

Collection Jacques Seligmann and Company, New York and Paris

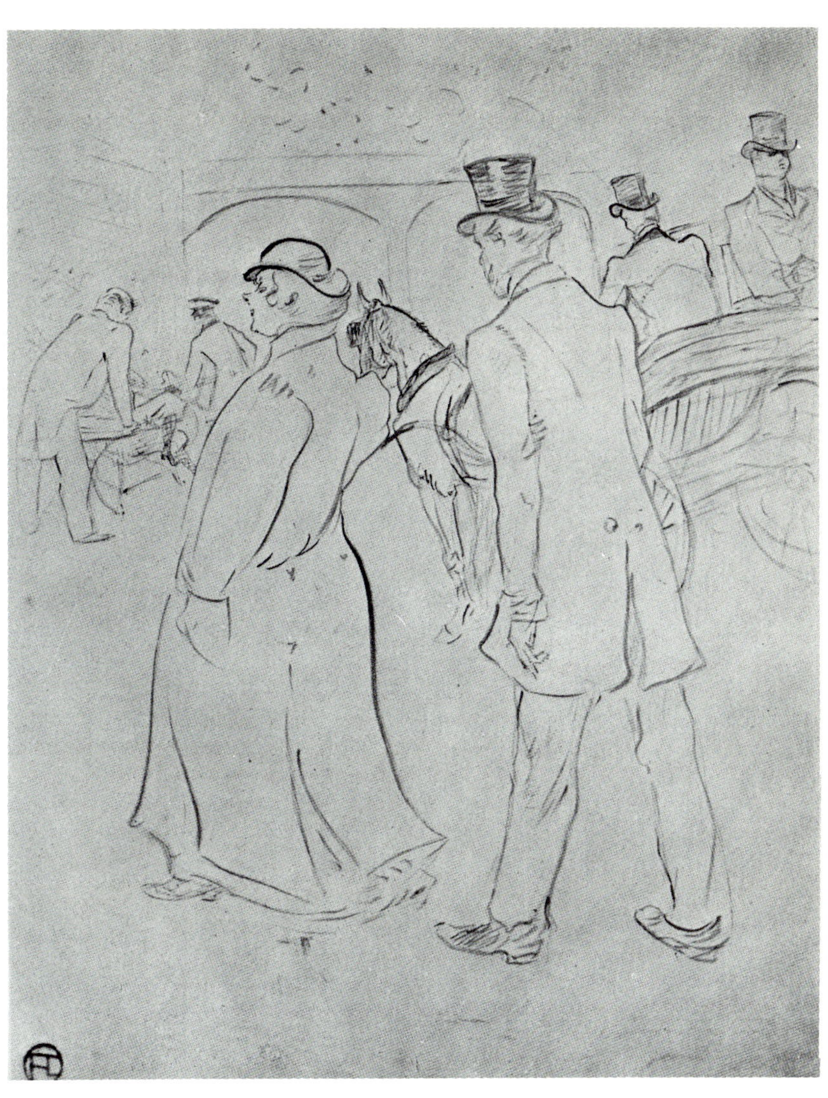

AT ARMENONVILLE (1896)

Chinese ink with touches of blue crayon on tan paper, 25½ x 19¾ inches
Collection The Minneapolis Institute of Arts (John de Laittre Memorial Collection)

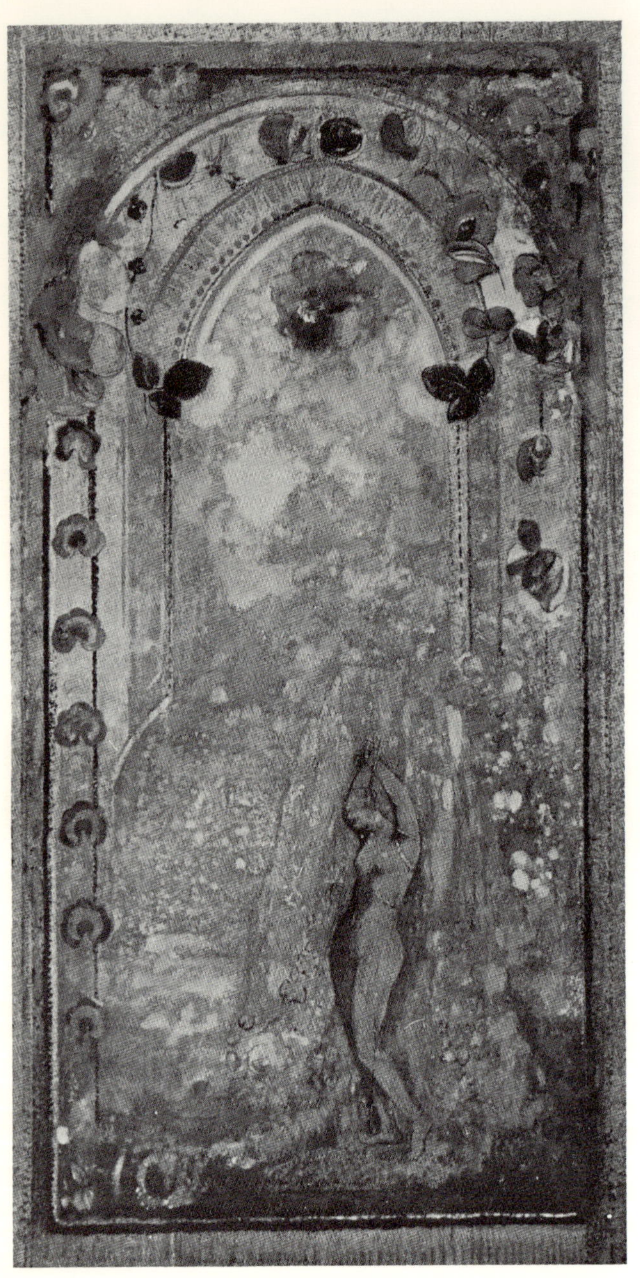

67 REDON

ANDROMEDA. *Oil, 69½ x 35¾ inches*
Collection C. W. Kraushaar, New York

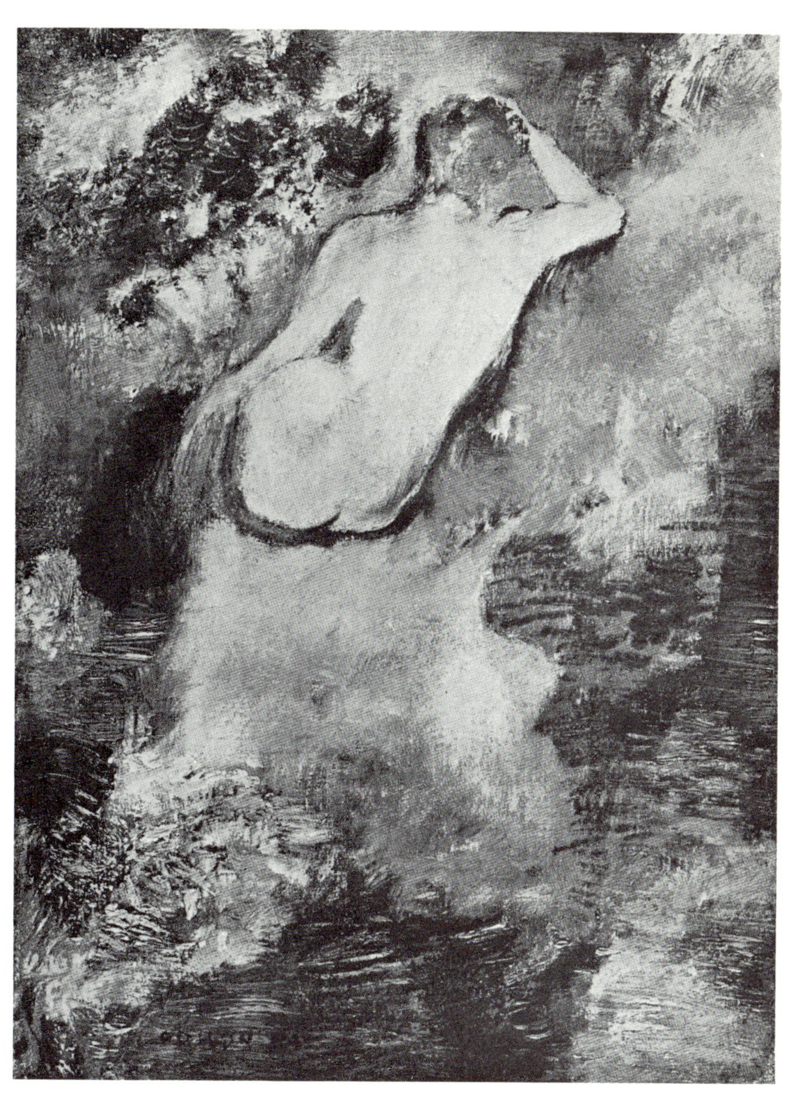

REDON 70
THE BIRTH OF VENUS. *Oil, 8¾ x 6 inches*
Collection Dr. B. D. Saklatwalla, Crafton, Pennsylvania

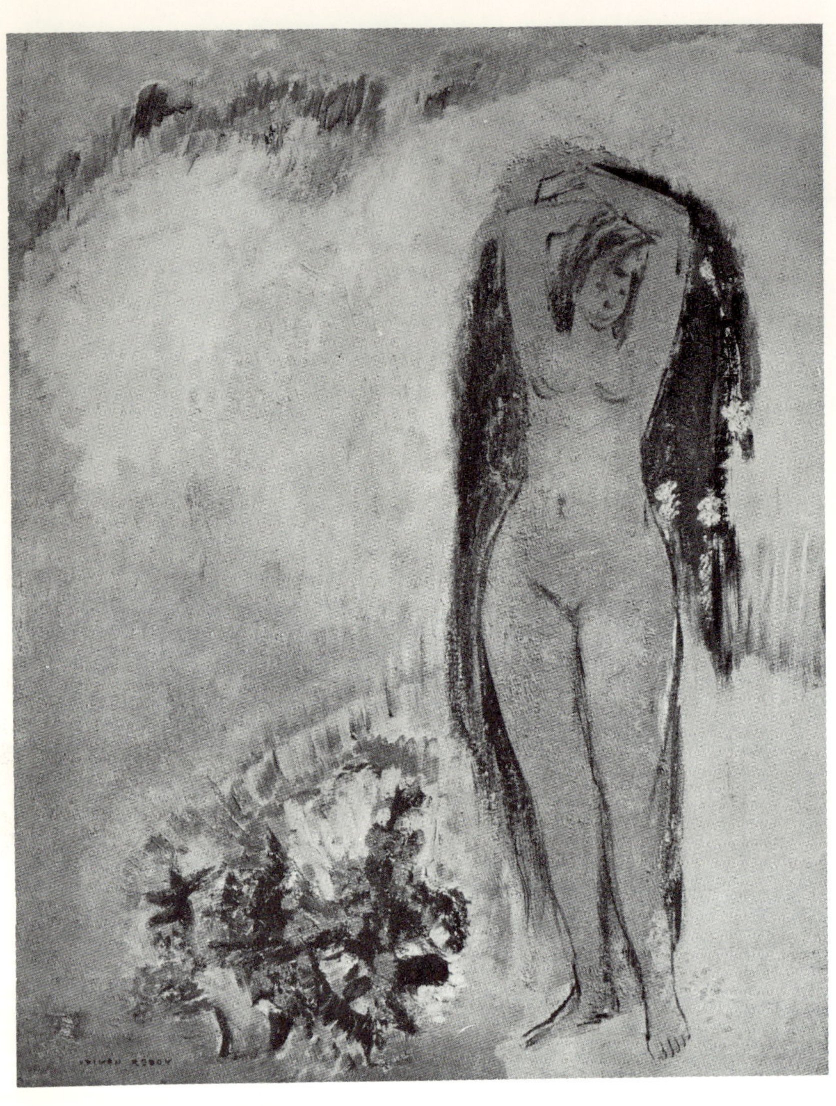

76 REDON

Apparition. *Oil, 15¼ x 12½ inches*
Collection Dr. W. R. Valentiner, Detroit

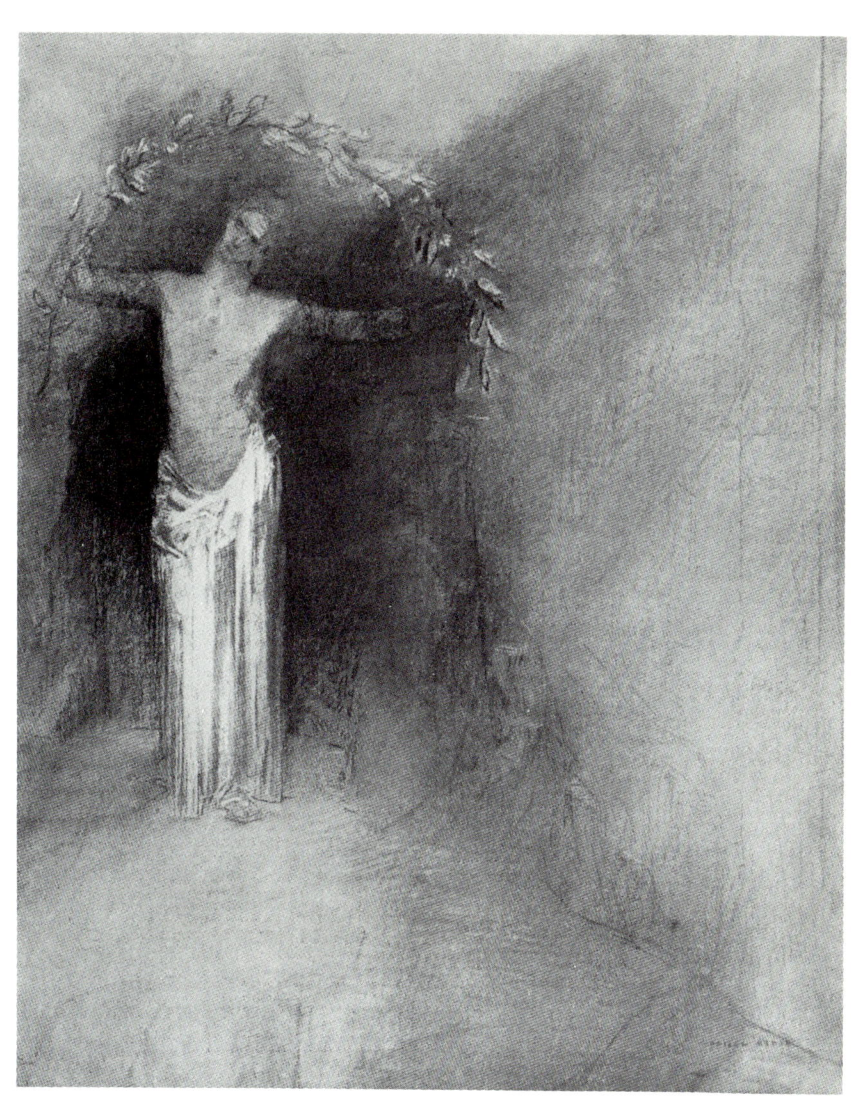

REDON 77
The Crown. *Pastel, 26 x 21 ¼ inches*
Collection Mrs. C. J. Martin, Minneapolis

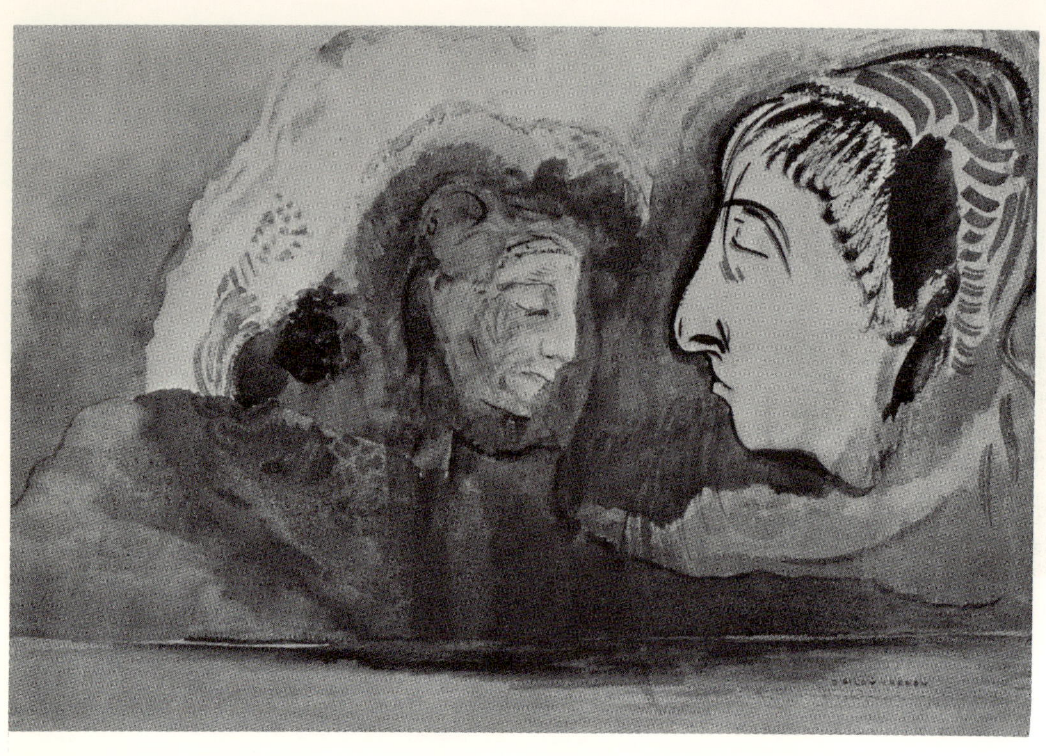

79 REDON

Dantesque Vision. *Watercolor, 19½ x 23 inches*
Collection John A. Holabird, Chicago

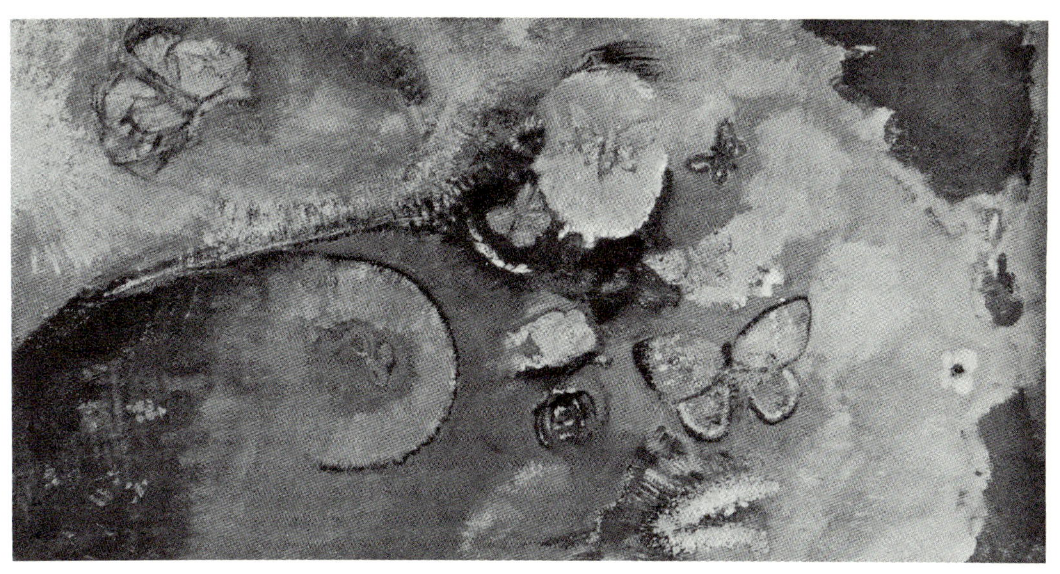

REDON 81

DREAM OF THE BUTTERFLIES. *Oil, 16 x 23¾ inches*
Collection The Detroit Institute of Arts

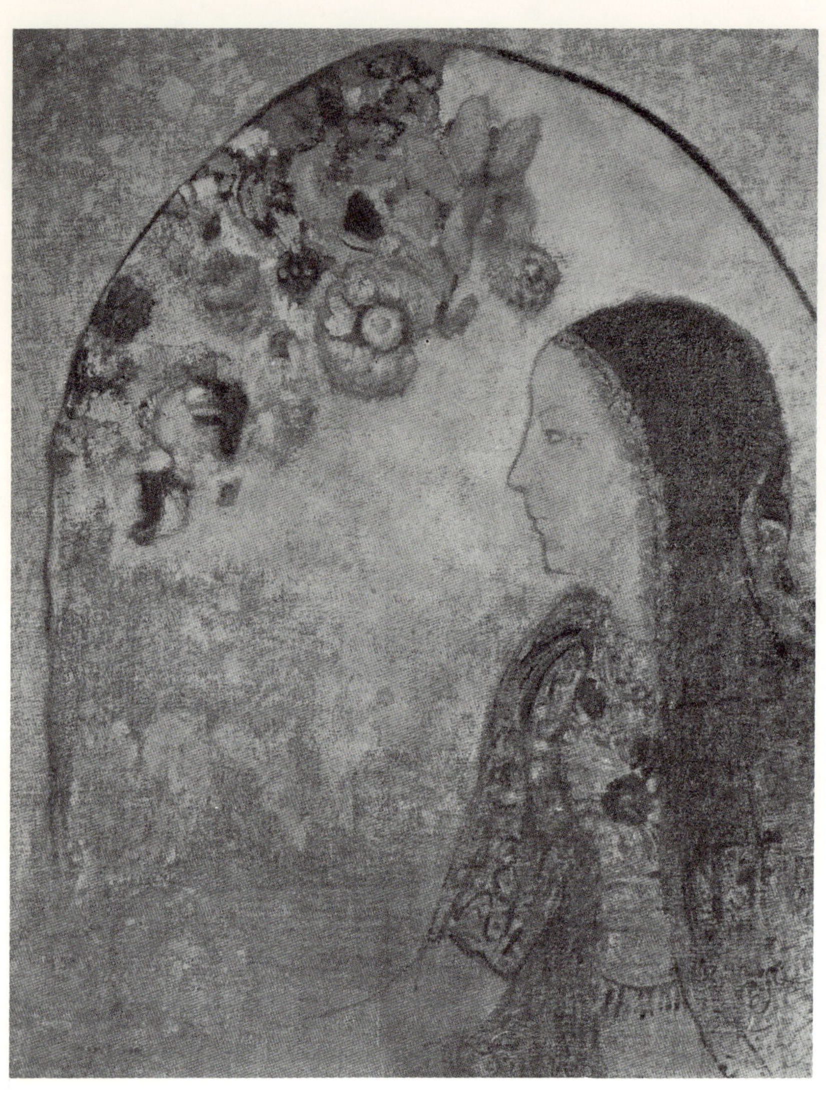

91 REDON

HEAD WITH FLOWERS. *Oil, 25¼ x 21¾ inches*
Collection M. B. Sanders, Jr., New York

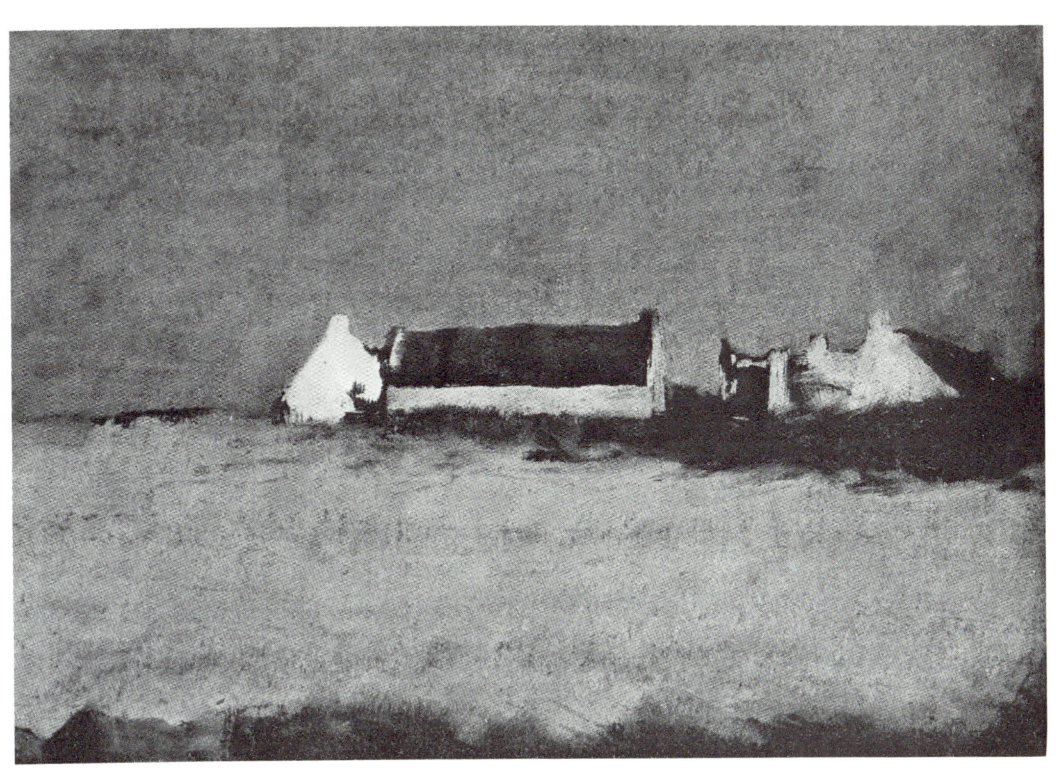

REDON 92

LANDSCAPE. *Oil 7 x 9½ inches*
Collection Mrs. Diodata O'Toole, New York

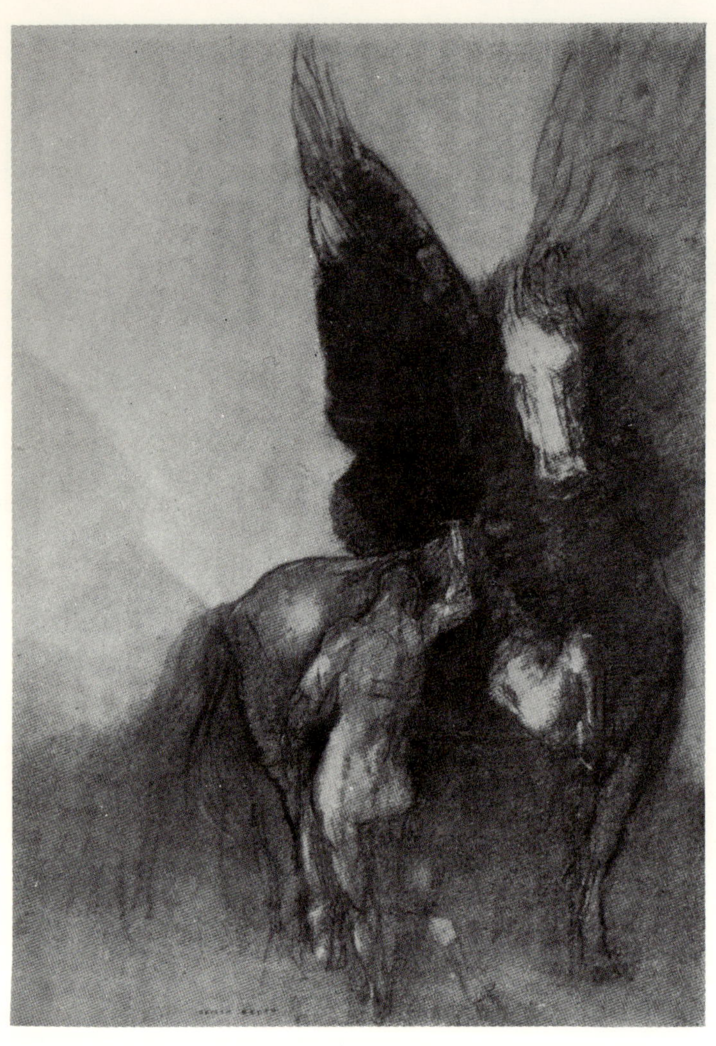

95 REDON

PEGASUS. *Drawing, 21 x 14 inches*
Collection Philip Hofer, New York

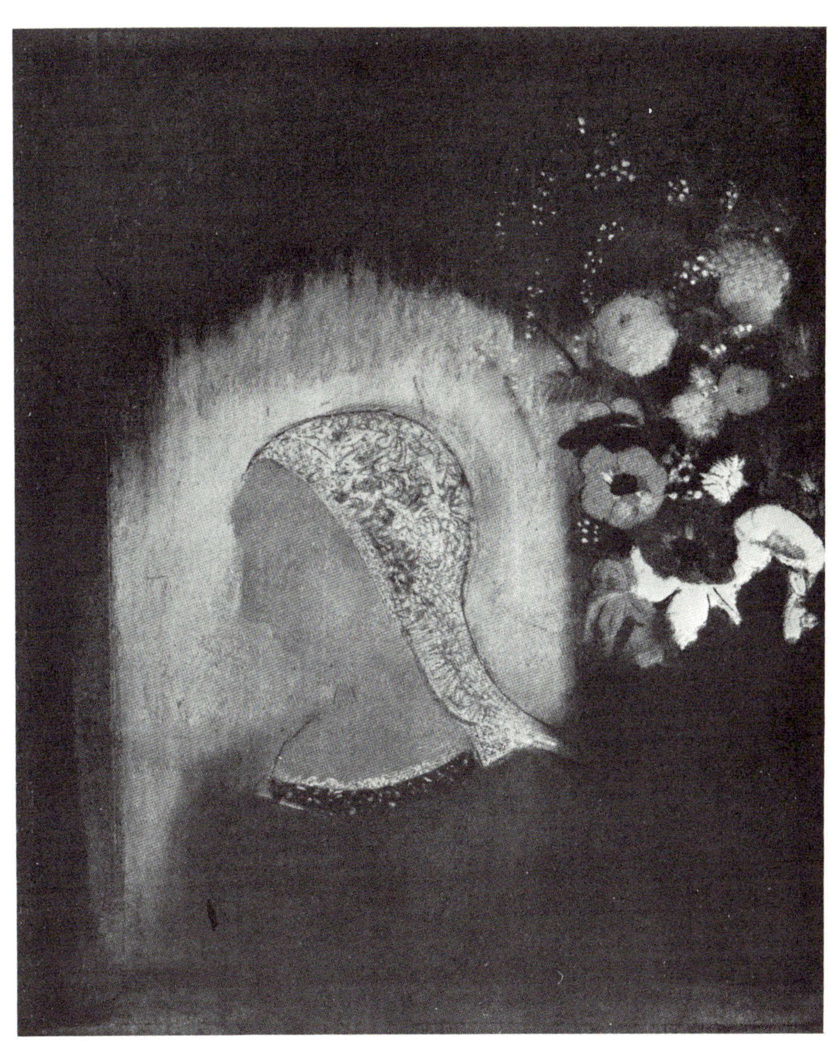

PROFILE AND FLOWERS. *Pastel, 27 ½ x 21 ½ inches*
Collection Jacques Seligmann and Company, New York and Paris

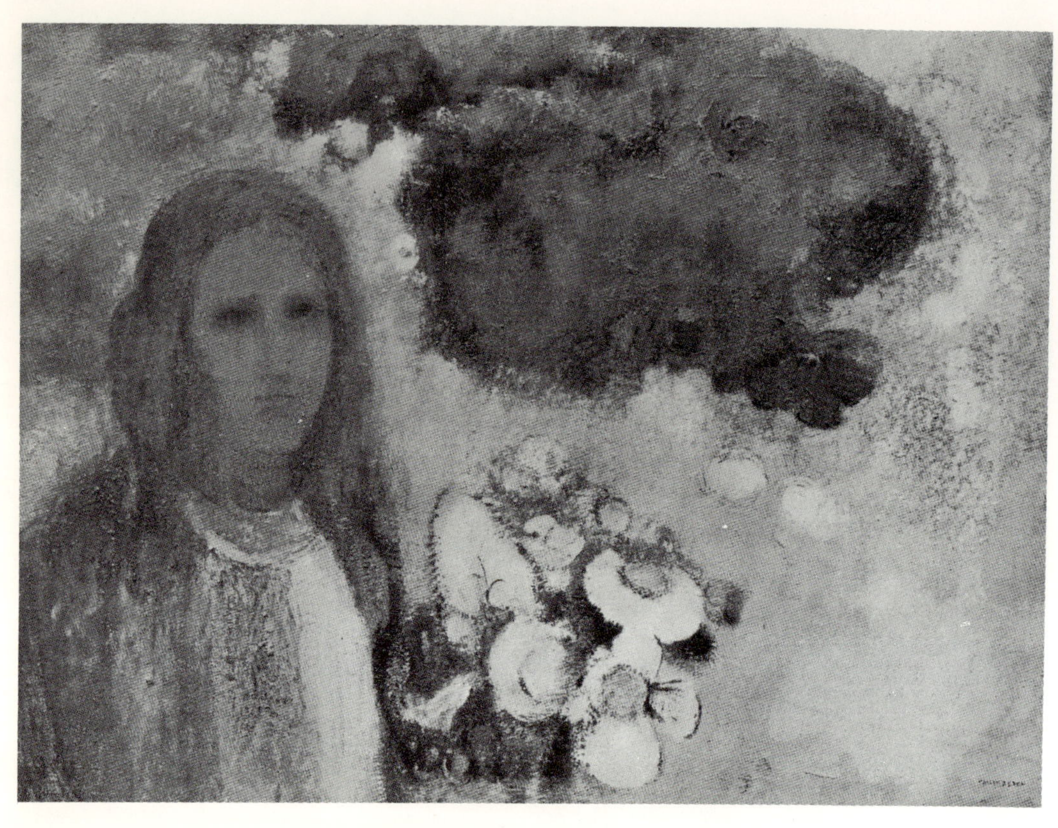

100 REDON

SPRING. *Oil, 21 x 29 inches*

Collection The Worcester Art Museum, Worcester

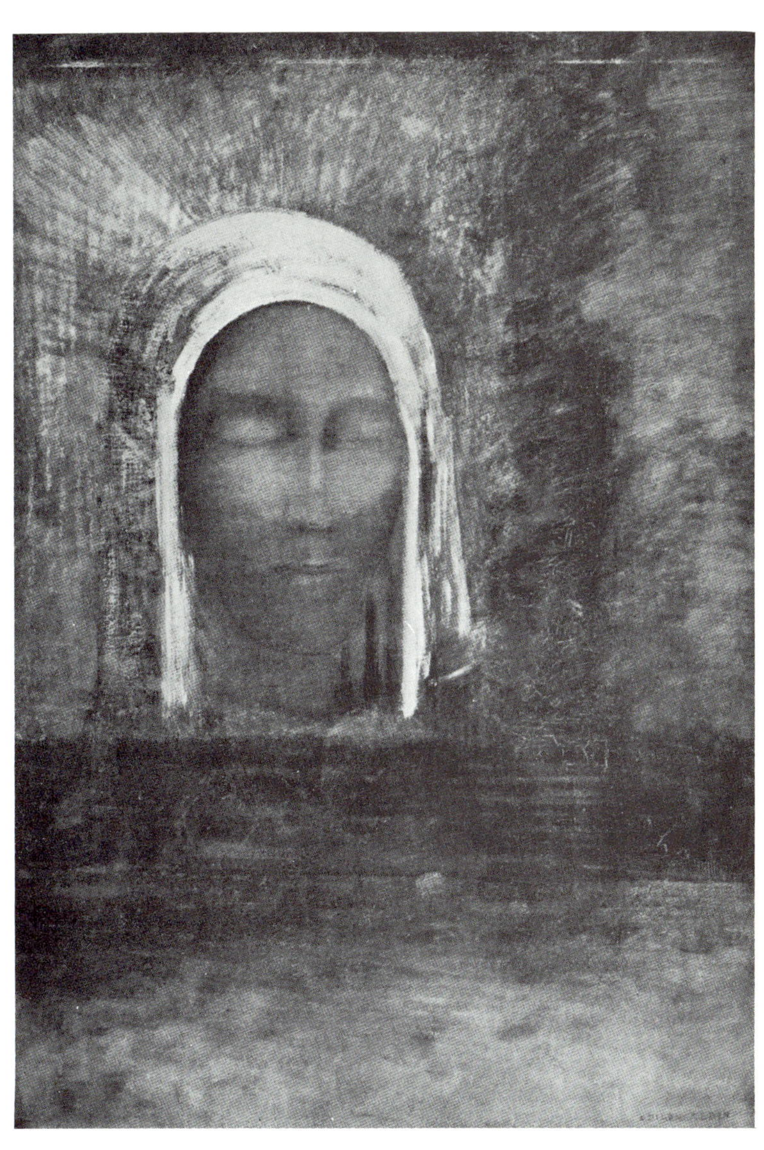

REDON 104

The Virgin. *Oil, 21 x 14½ inches*
Collection James W. Barney, New York
Courtesy The Art Museum of Yale University

ONE THOUSAND COPIES OF THIS CATALOG WERE
PRINTED FOR THE TRUSTEES OF THE MUSEUM OF
MODERN ART, BY THE PLANDOME PRESS OF NEW
YORK, FEBRUARY FIRST, NINETEEN THIRTY-ONE